World Famous
Mysterious
Objects

Vikas Khatri

PUSTAK MAHAL®

Publishers
Pustak Mahal®

J-3/16 , Daryaganj, New Delhi-110002
☎ 23276539, 23272783, 23272784 • *Fax:* 011-23260518
E-mail: info@pustakmahal.com • *Website:* www.pustakmahal.com

Sales Centre

- 10-B, Netaji Subhash Marg, Daryaganj, New Delhi-110002
  ☎ 23268292, 23268293, 23279900 • *Fax:* 011-23280567
  E-mail: rapidexdelhi@indiatimes.com
- 6686, Khari Baoli, Delhi-110006
  ☎ 23944314, 23911979

Branches

Bengaluru: ☎ 080-22234025 • *Telefax:* 080-22240209
E-mail: pustak@airtelmail.in • pustak@sancharnet.in
Mumbai: ☎ 022-22010941, 022-22053387
E-mail: rapidex@bom5.vsnl.net.in
Patna: ☎ 0612-3294193 • *Telefax:* 0612-2302719
E-mail: rapidexptn@rediffmail.com
Hyderabad: *Telefax:* 040-24737290
E-mail: pustakmahalhyd@yahoo.co.in

© **Pustak Mahal, New Delhi**

ISBN 978-81-223-1356-7

Edition: 2012

Printed at : **Unique Colour Cartoon, Delhi**

Introduction

Official position of science presents the picture of the past in which humanity started from primitive beginnings, and steadily progressed upward in the development of culture and science.

Most of the objects/artifacts preserved in archaeological and geological records have been neatly arranged to fit this accepted linear view of our past. Yet many other unearthed mysterious objects or "out-of-place artifacts" create obvious contradictions to the conservative picture of antiquity. They don't fit the established pattern of prehistory, pointing back instead to the existence of advanced civilizations before any of the known ancient cultures came into being.

Though such discoveries are well-documented, most historians would like to sweep these disturbing anomalies under the proverbial rug.

In addition, the mysterious objects or artifacts seem to confirm ancient legends and stories describing human history affected by a very advanced earthly civilization perished in a global cataclysm or influenced by extraterrestrial gods.

In this book, a wide and varied range of mysterious objects are surveyed to take us on a lengthy but intriguing research journey through history and the contemporary world.

These investigations in the world of mysterious object are intriguing and fascinating, and I feel great pleasure in sharing the research data – and a few theories – with my readers.

Contents

Vimana: Ancient Indian Aircraft

Vimana is a Sanskrit word with several meanings ranging from temple or palace to mythological flying machines described in Sanskrit epics. Some modern UFO enthusiasts (like Desmond Leslie, co-author with George Adamski, in 1953, of one of the first books on UFOs entitled *Flying Saucers Have Landed*) have pointed to the Vimana as evidence for advanced technological civilizations in the distant past, or as support for ancient astronaut theories. Others have linked the flying machines to the legend of the Nine Unknown Men. Many researchers into the UFO enigma tend to overlook a very important fact. While it assumed that most flying saucers are of alien, or perhaps Governmental Military origin, another possible origin of UFOs is ancient India and Atlantis. Informations about Ancient Indian flying vehicles comes from ancient Indian sources; written texts that have come down to us through the centuries. There is no doubt that most of these texts are authentic; many are the well known ancient Indian Epics themselves, and there are literally hundreds of them. Most of them have not even been translated into English yet from the old Sanskrit.

The Indian Emperor Ashoka started a "Secret Society of the Nine Unknown Men": great Indian scientists who were supposed to catalogue the many sciences. Ashoka kept their work secret because he was afraid that the advanced science catalogued by these men, culled from ancient Indian sources, would be used for the evil purpose of war, which Ashoka was strongly against, having been converted to Buddhism after defeating a rival army in a bloody battle. The "Nine Unknown Men" wrote a total of nine books, presumably one each. Book number one was "*The Secrets of Gravitation*!". This book, known to historians, but not actually seen by them dealt chiefly with "gravity control." It is presumably still around somewhere, kept in a secret library in India, Tibet or elsewhere (perhaps even in North America somewhere). One can certainly understand Ashoka's reasoning for wanting to keep such knowledge a secret, assuming it

ASHOKA. GLANDSON OF 5 KING GUPTA DEFEATED
PERSIAN KING DARIUS AT CALINGA.

exists. If the Nazis had such weapons at their disposal during World War II, Ashoka was also aware devastating wars using such advanced vehicles and other "futuristic weapons" that had destroyed the ancient Indian "Rama Empire" several thousand years before.

Few years ago, the Chinese discovered some Sanskrit documents in Lhasa, Tibet and sent them to the University of Chandrigarh to be translated. Dr. Ruth Reyna of the University said recently that the documents contain directions for building interstellar spaceships! Their method of propulsion, she said, was "anti-gravitational" and was based upon a system analogous to that of "laghima," the unknown power of the ego existing in man's physiological makeup, "a centrifugal force strong enough to counteract all gravitational pull."

According to Hindu Yogis, it is this "laghima" which enables a person to levitate. Dr. Reyna said that on board these machines, which were called "Astras" by the text, the ancient Indians could have sent a detachment of men onto any planet, according to the document, which is thought to be thousands of years old. The manuscripts were also said to reveal the secret of "antima", "the cap of invisibility" and "garima", "how to become as heavy as a mountain of lead."

Naturally, Indian scientists did not take the texts very seriously, but then became more positive about the value of them when the Chinese announced that they were including certain parts of the data for study in their space program! This was one of the first instances of a government admitting to be researching anti-gravity. The manuscripts did not say definitely that interplanetary travel was ever made but did mention, of all things, a planned trip to the Moon, though it is not clear whether this trip was actually carried out.

However, one of the great Indian epics, the Ramayana, does have a highly detailed story in it of a trip to the moon in a Vimana (or "Astra"), and in fact details a battle on the moon with an "Asvin" (or "Atlantean" airship.) This is but a small bit of recent evidence of anti-gravity and aerospace technology used by Indians. To really understand the technology, we must go much further back in time. The so-called "Rama Empire" of Northern India and Pakistan developed at least fifteen thousand years ago on the Indian sub-continent and was a nation of many large, sophisticated cities, many of which are still to

6

be found in the deserts of Pakistan, northern, and western India. Rama existed, apparently, parallel to the Atlantean civilization in the mid-Atlantic Ocean, and was ruled by "enlightened Priest-Kings" who governed the cities.

The seven greatest capital cities of Rama were known in classical Hindu texts as "*The Seven Rishi Cities.*" The Ramayana describes a Vimana as a double-deck, circular (cylindrical) aircraft with portholes and a dome. It flew with the speed of the wind and gave forth a melodious sound (a humming noise). Ancient Indian texts on Vimanas are so numerous it would take several books to relate what they have to say. The ancient Indians themselves wrote entire flight manuals on the control of various types of Vimanas, of which there were basically four: the Shakuna Vimana, the Sundara Vimana, the Rukma Vimana and the Tripura Vimana.

The Samara Sutradhara is a scientific treatise dealing with every possible angle of air travel in a Vimana. There are 230 stanzas dealing with the construction, take-off, cruising for thousand of miles, normal and forced landings, and even possible collisions with birds. In 1875, the Vaimanika Sastra, a fourth century B.C. text written by Bharadvajy the Wise, using even older texts as his source, was rediscovered in a temple in India. It dealt with the operation of Vimanas and included information on the steering, precautions for long flights, protection of the airships from storms and lightening and how to switch the drive to "solar energy" from a free energy source which sounds like "anti-gravity."

The *Vaimanika Sastra* (or Vymaanika-Shaastra) has eight chapters with diagrams, describing three types of aircraft, including apparatuses that could neither catch on fire nor break. It also mentions 31 essential parts of these vehicles and 16 materials from which they are constructed, which absorb light and heat; for which reason they were considered suitable for the construction of Vimanas.

This document has been translated into English: Vymaanida-shaastra Aeronautics by Maharishi Bharadwaaja, translated into English and edited, printed and published by Mr. G. R. Josyer, Mysore, India, 1979. Mr. Josyer is the director of the International Academy of Sanskrit Investigation located in Mysore. There seems to be no doubt that Vimanas were powered by some sort of "anti-gravity." Vimanas

7

took off vertically, and were capable of hovering in the sky, like a modern helicopter or dirigible. Bharadvajy the Wise refers to no less than 70 authorities and 10 experts of air travel in antiquity. These sources are now lost. Vimanas were kept in a Vimana Griha, a kind of hanger, and were sometimes said to be propelled by a yellowish-white liquid, and sometimes by some sort of mercury compound, though writers seem confused in this matter.

SHAKUNA VIMANA

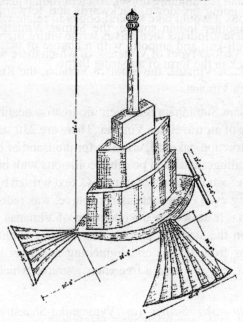

PERSPECTIVE VIEW

Dream by

T.K. ELLAPPA,
Bangalore,
2-12-1925

Prepared under instruction of

Pandit SUBBARAYA SASTRY,
of Anekal, Bangalore.

It is most likely that the later writers on Vimanas, wrote as observers and from earlier texts, and were understandably confused on the principle of their propulsion. The "yellowish-white liquid" sounds suspiciously like gasoline, and perhaps Vimanas had a number of different propulsion sources, including combustion engines and even "pulse-jet" engines. It is interesting to note, that

8

the Nazis developed the first practical pulse-jet engines for their V-8 rocket "buzz bombs." Hitler and the Nazi staff were exceptionally interested in ancient India and Tibet and sent expeditions to both these places yearly, starting in the 30's, in order to gather esoteric evidence that they did so, and perhaps it was from these people that the Nazis gained some of their scientific information! According to the Dronaparva, part of the Mahabarata, and the Ramayana, one Vimana described was shaped like a sphere and born along at great speed on a mighty wind generated by mercury. It moved like a UFO, going up, down, backwards and forwards as the pilot desired. In another Indian source, the Samar, Vimanas were, "iron machines, well-knit and smooth, with a charge of mercury that shot out of the back in the form of a roaring flame."

Sanskrit texts are filled with references to Gods who fought battles in the sky using Vimanas equipped with weapons as deadly as any we can deploy in these more enlightened times. For example, there is a passage in the Ramayana which reads: The Puspaka car that resembles the Sun and belongs to my brother was brought by the powerful Ravan; that aerial and excellent car going everywhere at will.... that car resembling a bright cloud in the sky. ".. and the King [Rama] got in, and the excellent car at the command of the Raghira, rose up into the higher atmosphere."

In the Mahabharatra, an ancient Indian poem of enormous length, we learn that an individual named Asura Maya had a Vimana measuring twelve cubits in circumference, with four strong wheels.

The poem is a veritable gold mine of information relating to conflicts between gods who settled their differences apparently using weapons as lethal as the ones we are capable of deploying.

Apart from 'blazing missiles', the poem records the use of other deadly weapons. 'Indra's Dart' operated via a circular 'reflector'. When switched on, it produced a 'shaft of light' which, when focused on any target, immediately 'consumed it with its power'.

In one particular exchange, the hero, Krishna, is pursuing his enemy, Salva, in the sky, when Salva's Vimana, the Saubha is made invisible in some way. Undeterred, Krishna immediately fires off a special weapon: 'I quickly laid on an arrow, which killed by seeking out sound.'

Many other terrible weapons are described, quite matter of factly, in the Mahabharata, but the most fearsome of all is the one used against the Vrishis. The narrative records: "Gurkha flying in his swift and powerful Vimana hurled against the three cities of the Vrishis and Andhakas a single projectile charged with all the power of the Universe. An incandescent column of smoke and fire, as brilliant as ten thousands suns, rose in all its splendor. It was the unknown weapon, the Iron Thunderbolt, a gigantic messenger of death which reduced to ashes the entire race of the Vrishnis and Andhakas." It is important to note, that these kinds of records are not isolated.

They can be cross-correlated with similiar reports in other ancient civilizations. The after-affects of this Iron Thunderbolt have an ominously recognizable ring. Apparently, those killed by it were so burnt that their corpses were unidentifiable. The survivors fared little better, as it caused their hair and nails to fall out. Perhaps the most disturbing and challenging, information about these allegedly mythical Vihmanas in the ancient records is that there are some matter-of-fact records, describing how to build one. In their way, the instructions are quite precise.

In the Sanskrit Samarangana Sutradhara, it is written: Strong and durable must the body of the Vihmana be made, like a great flying bird of light material. Inside one must put the mercury engine with its iron heating apparatus underneath. By means of the power latent in the mercury which sets the driving whirlwind in motion, a man sitting inside may travel a great distance in the sky. The movements of the Vimana are such that it can vertically ascend, vertically descend, move slanting forwards and backwards. With the help of the machines human beings can fly in the air and heavenly beings can come down to earth. It is possible that mercury did have something to do with the propulsion, or more possibly, with the guidance system.

Curiously, Soviet scientists have discovered what they call "age-old instruments used in navigating cosmic vehicles" in caves in Turkestan and the Gobi Desert. The "devices" are hemispherical objects of glass or porcelain, ending in a cone with a drop of mercury inside. It is evident that ancient Indians flew around in these vehicles, all over Asia, to Atlantis presumably; and even, apparently, to South America. Writing found at Mohenjodaro in Pakistan (presumed to be one of the "Seven Rishi Cities of the Rama Empire") and still undeciphered, has also been found in one other place in the world: Easter Island! Writing on Easter Island, called Rongo-Rongo writing, is also undeciphered, and is uncannily similar to the Mohenjodaro script. Was Easter Island an air base for the Rama Empire's Vimana route?

In Tibet, no small distance, and speaks of the "fiery chariot" thusly: "Bhima flew along in his car, resplendent as the sun and loud as thunder... The flying chariot shone like a flame in the night sky of summer ... it swept by like a comet... It was as if two suns were shining. Then the chariot rose up and all the heaven brightened."

In the Mahavira of Bhavabhuti, a Jain text of the eighth century culled from older texts and traditions, we read: "An aerial chariot, the Pushpaka, conveys many people to the capital of Ayodhya. The sky is full of stupendous flying-machines, dark as night, but picked out by lights with a yellowish glare."

The Vedas, ancient Hindu poems, thought to be the oldest of all the Indian texts, describe Vimanas of various shapes and sizes: the "ahnihotra-vimana" with two engines, the "elephant-vimana" with more engines, and other types named after the kingfisher, ibis and other animals. Unfortunately, Vimanas, like most scientific discoveries, were ultimately used for war.

Atlanteans used their flying machines, "Vailixi," a similar type of aircraft, to literally try and subjugate the world, it would seem, if Indian texts are to be believed. The Atlanteans, known as "Asvins" in the Indian writings, were apparently even more advanced technologically

11

than the Indians, and certainly of a more war-like temperament. Although no ancient texts on Atlantean Vailixi are known to exist, some information has come down through esoteric, "occult" sources which describe their flying machines. Similar, if not identical to Vimanas, Vailixi were generally "cigar shaped" and had the capability of maneuvering underwater as well as in the atmosphere or even outer space.

Other vehicles, like Vimanas, were saucer shaped, and could apparently also be submerged. According to Eklal Kueshana, author of *"The Ultimate Frontier,"* in an article he wrote in 1966, Vailixi were first developed in Atlantis 20,000 years ago, and the most common ones are, "saucer-shaped of generally trapezoidal cross-section with three hemispherical engine pods on the underside." "They use a mechanical antigravity device driven by engines developing approximately 80,000 horse power."

The Hakatha (Laws of the Babylonians) states quite unambiguously: The privilege of operating a flying machine is great. The knowledge of flight is among the most ancient of our inheritances. A gift from 'those from upon high'. We received it from them as a means of saving many lives. More fantastic still is the information given in the ancient Chaldean work, The Sifrala, which contains over one hundred pages of technical details on building a flying machine. It contains words which translate as graphite rod, copper coils, crystal indicator, vibrating spheres, stable angles, etc. The Ramayana, Mahabarata and other texts speak of the hideous war that took place, some ten or twelve thousand years ago between Atlantis and Rama using weapons of destruction that could not be imagined by readers until the second half of this century. The ancient Mahabharata, one of the sources on Vimanas, goes on to tell the awesome destructiveness of the war:

"A single projectile charged with all the power of the Universe. An incandescent column of smoke and flame as bright as the thousand suns rose in all its splendor ... An iron thunderbolt, a gigantic messenger of death, which reduced to ashes the entire race of the Vrishnis and the Andhakas. ... the corpses were so burned as to be unrecognizable. The hair and nails fell out; Pottery broke without apparent cause, and the birds turned white. ... After a few hours all foodstuffs were infected...

... to escape from this fire the soldiers threw themselves in streams to wash themselves and their equipment..."

It would seem that the Mahabharata is describing an atomic war! References like this one are not isolated; but battles, using a fantastic array of weapons and aerial vehicles are common in all the epic Indian books. One even describes a Vimana-Vailix battle on the Moon! The above section very accurately describes what an atomic explosion would look like and the effects of the radioactivity on the population. Jumping into water is the only respite.

When the Rishi City of Mohenjodaro was excavated by archeologists in the last century, they found skeletons just lying in the streets, some of them holding hands, as if some great doom had suddenly overtaken them. These skeletons are among the most radioactive ever found, on a par with those found at Hiroshima and Nagasaki. Ancient cities whose brick and stone walls have literally been vitrified, that is–fused together, can be found in India, Ireland, Scotland, France, Turkey and other places.

TRIPURA VIMANA

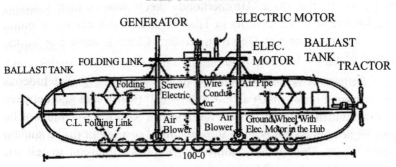

There is no logical explanation for the vitrification of stone forts and cities, except from an atomic blast. Furthermore, at Mohenjo-Daro, a well planned city laid on a grid, with a plumbing system superior to those used in Pakistan and India today, the streets were littered with "black lumps of glass." These globs of glass were discovered to be clay pots that had melted under intense heat! With the cataclysmic sinking of Atlantis and the wiping out of Rama with atomic weapons, the world collapsed into a "stone age" of sorts, and modern history

13

picks up a few thousand years later. Yet, it would seem that not all the Vimanas and Vailixi of Rama and Atlantis were gone.

Built to last for thousands of years, many of them would still be in use, as evidenced by Ashoka's "Nine Unknown Men" and the Lhasa manuscript. That secret societies or "Brotherhoods" of exceptional, "enlightened" human beings would have preserved these inventions and the knowledge of science, history, etc., does not seem surprising. Many well known historical personages including Jesus, Buddha, Lao Tzu, Confucius, Krishna, Zoroaster, Mahavira, Quetzalcoatl, Akhenaton, Moses, and more recent inventors and of course many other people who will probably remain anonymous, were probably members of such a secret organization. It is interesting to note that when Alexander the Great invaded India more than two thousand years ago, his historians chronicled that at one point they were attacked by "flying, fiery shields" that dove at his army and frightened the cavalry.

These "flying saucers" did not use any atomic bombs or beam weapons on Alexander's army however, perhaps out of benevolence, and Alexander went on to conquer India. It has been suggested by many writers that these "Brotherhoods" keep some of their Vimanas and Vailixi in secret caverns in Tibet or some other place is Central Asia, and the Lop Nor Desert in western China is known to be the centre of a great UFO mystery.

Perhaps it is here that many of the airships are still kept, in underground bases much as the Americans, British and Soviets have built around the world in the past few decades. Still, not all UFO activity can be accounted for by old Vimanas making trips to the Moon for some reason. Undoubtedly, some ire from the Military Governments of the world, and possibly even from other planets.

Voynich Manuscript

The Voynich Manuscript has been dubbed "The Most Mysterious
Manuscript in the World". It is named after its discoverer, the
American antique book dealer and collector, Wilfrid M. Voynich, who
discovered it in 1912, amongst a collection of ancient manuscripts
kept in villa Mondragone in Frascati, near Rome, which had been by
then turned into a Jesuit College (closed in 1953). Some believe it to
be a book about alchemy. The Voynich manuscript is a mysterious
illustrated book with incomprehensible contents. It is thought to have
been written approximately 400 years ago by an unknown author in an
unidentified script and unintelligible language. As of 2005, the Voynich
manuscript is item MS 408 in the Beinecke Rare Book Library of Yale
University. The first facsimile edition was published in 2005.

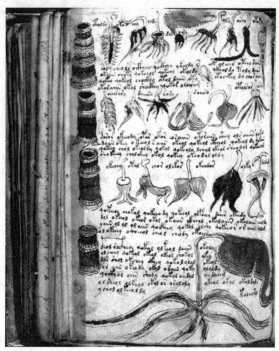

Over its recorded existence, the Voynich manuscript has been the object of intense study by many professional and amateur cryptographers, including some top American and British codebreakers of World War II fame (all of whom failed to decipher a single word). This string of failures has turned the Voynich manuscript into a famous subject of historical cryptology, but it has also given weight to the theory that the book is simply an elaborate hoax – a meaningless sequence of arbitrary symbols. No one knows the origins of the manuscript. Experts believe it is European based on the drawings. They believe it was written in between the 15th and 17th centuries. The manuscript is small, seven by ten inches, but thick, nearly 235 pages.

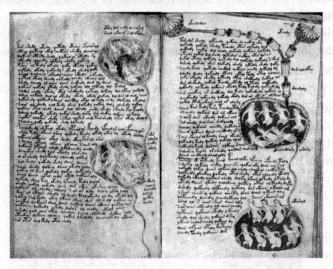

It is an alphabetic script, but of an alphabet variously reckoned to have from nineteen to twenty-eight letters, none of which bear any relationship to any English or European letter system. The text has no apparent corrections. There is evidence for two different "languages" (investigated by Currier and D'Imperio) and more than one scribe, probably indicating an ambiguous coding scheme.

Apparently, Voynich wanted to have the mysterious manuscript deciphered and provided photographic copies to a number of experts. However, despite the efforts of many well-known cryptologists and scholars, the book remains unread. There are some claims of decipherment, but to date, none of these can be substantiated with a complete translation. The book was bought by H. P. Kraus (a New York book antiquarian) in 1961 for the sum of $24,500. He later valued it at $160,000 but was unable to find a buyer. Finally he donated it to Yale University in 1969, where it remains to date at the Beinecke Rare Book Library with catalogue number MS 408. It is known (from a letter of Johannes Marcus Marci to Athanasius Kircher dated 1666) that the manuscript was bought by Emperor Rudolph II of Bohemia (1552-1612).

Historically, it first appears in 1586 at the court of Rudolph II of Bohemia, who was one of the most eccentric European monarchs of that or any other period. Rudolph collected dwarfs and had a regiment of giants in his army. He was surrounded by astrologers, and he was fascinated by games and codes and music. He was typical of the occult-oriented, Protestant noblemen of this period and epitomized the liberated northern European prince. He was a patron of alchemy and supported the printing of alchemical literature.

The Rosicrucian conspiracy was being quietly fomented during this same period. To Rudolph's court came an unknown person who sold this manuscript to the king for three hundred gold ducats, which, translated into modern monetary units, is about fourteen thousand dollars. This is an astonishing amount of money to have paid for a manuscript at that time, which indicated that the Emperor must have been highly impressed by it.

Accompanying the manuscript was a letter that stated that it was the work of the Englishman Roger Bacon, who flourished in the thirteenth century and who was a noted pre-Copernican astronomer. Only two years before the appearance of the Voynich Manuscript, John Dee, the great English navigator, astrologer, magician, intelligence agent, and occultist had lectured in Prague on Bacon.

The manuscript somehow passed to Jacobus de Tepenecz, the director of Rudolph's botanical gardens (his signature is present in folio 1r) and it is speculated that this must have happened after 1608, when Jacobus Horcicki received his title 'de Tepenecz'. Thus 1608 is the earliest definite date for the Manuscript.

Codes from the early sixteenth century onward in Europe were all derived from The Stenographica of Johannes Trethemius, Bishop of Sponheim, an alchemist who wrote on the encripherment of secret messages. He had a limited number of methods, and no military, alchemical, religious, or political code was composed by any other means throughout a period that lasted well into the seventeenth century. Yet the Voynich Manuscript does not appear to have any relationship to the codes derivative of Johannes Trethemius, Bishop of Sponheim.

In 1622 and the manuscript passed to the possession of an unidentified individual that left the book in his/her will to Marci. Marci must have known about this manuscript before 1644, as the information concerning the price that the Emperor paid came from Dr. Raphael Missowski (1580-1644) (as mentioned in his letter).

Marci sent the manuscript immediately with the letter to Athanasius Kircher (a Jesuit priest and scholar in Rome) in 1666 who apparently also knew of it and had exchanged letters and transcribed portions with the previous unidentified owner.

Between that time and 1912 (when Voynich discovered it) it is speculated that the manuscript may have been stored or forgotten in some library and finally moved to the Jesuit College at the Villa Mondragone. Marci's letter to Kircher was still attached to the manuscript when Voynich bought it.

In that letter, Marci mentioned the name of Roger Bacon (1214-1292) as a possible author, although no conclusive evidence of authorship is available. A possible link between Rudolph and Bacon is John Dee (an English mathematician and astrologer, collector of Bacon's work) who visited Rudolph's court in 1582-86.

The Veronica's Veil

Christian legend tells of a fabled, linen veil which inexplicably shows the face of Jesus. The veil has more intriguing mysteries surrounding it than just what caused the image. The Vatican claims it has been holding the cloth in its archive continuously since the twelfth century. According to legend, a woman from Jerusalem encountered Jesus along the Via Dolorosa on the way to Calvary. When she paused to wipe the sweat (Latin suda) off his face with her veil, his image was imprinted on the cloth. The woman's name was Veronica, she is said to have kept the cloth and realised that it had holy healing powers.

However there is no reference to the story of Veronica and her veil in the canonical Gospels. The closest is the miracle of the woman who was healed by touching the hem of Jesus' garment (Luke 8:43-48); her name is later identified as Veronica by the apocryphal "Acts of Pilate". According to some versions, Veronica later travelled to Rome where she used it to cure Emperor Tiberius of a malady, and then left it in the care of Pope Clement and the Catholic Church.

It has often been assumed that the Veronica was present in the old St Peter's in the papacy of John VII (705-8) as a chapel known as the Veronica chapel was built during his reign, and this seems to have been the assumption of later writers. This is far from certain however as mosaics

19

which decorated that chapel do not refer to the Veronica story in any way. Furthermore, contemporaneous writers make no reference to the Veronica in this period. It would appear however that the Veronica was in place by 1011 when a scribe was identified as keeper of the cloth. However, firm recording of the Veronica only begins in 1199 when two pilgrims named Gerald de Barri (Giraldus Cambrensis) and Gervase of Tilbury made two accounts at different times of a visit to Rome which made direct reference to the existence of the Veronica. Shortly after that, in 1207, the cloth became more prominent when it was publicly paraded and displayed by Pope Innocent III, who also granted indulgences to anyone praying before it. This parade, between St Peter's and The Santo Spirito Hospital, became an annual event and on one such occasion in 1300 Pope Boniface VIII, who had it translated to St. Peter's in 1297, was inspired to proclaim the first Jubilee in 1300. During this Jubilee the Veronica's Veil was publicly displayed and became one of the "Mirabilia Urbis" ("wonders of the City") for the pilgrims who visited Rome.

In 1608 the area of the Basilica displaying the veil was demolished in order to be redesigned, and the cloth was placed in the Vatican's archives. Under tight security, it was brought out once a year for public viewing.

On 3rd June 1999, Professor Heinrich Pfeiffer, a Professor of Early Christian Art at the Pontifical Gregorian University in Rome, and official advisor to the Papal Commission for the Cultural History of the Church, revealed he had successfully completed a 13-year investigation to find the real Veil of Veronica. He explained that the artefact annually displayed was merely a copy that the Vatican had created so as not to disappoint pilgrims. He claimed to have actually found the true relic in an abbey in the tiny village of Manopello, high in the Italian Apennine mountains.

Professor Pfeiffer says that during a rebuilding of St. Peter's Basilica between 1506-1626, at one point involving Michelangelo who designed the Dome, the Veil was stolen from the Vatican and brought, eventually, to Manoppello. The claim is made that in 1506 during construction of the new St. Peter's Basilica, (as recorded in the Capucine Provincial Archive) – a mysterious stranger brought the Veil to Manoppello and gave it to a gentleman of the place, Dr.

20

Giacomo Antonio Leonelli. The precious veil was kept in the Leonelli family for over a century. Then, in 1608, it was included in the nuptial gifts for Maria Leonelli for 400 scudi (an old Italian unit of currency), but the gift was never delivered. In 1608 Maria's husband, Pancrazio Petrucci stole it from his father-in-law's home. Later, in order to have her husband released from prison in Chieti, she sold the veil to Dr. Donato Antonio De Fabritis who placed it in a Walnut Frame adorned with Silver and gold between two pieces of glass and presented it to the Capuchins in 1638 who have kept it in the monastery and revered it as a sacred icon ever since, as recorded between 1640 and 1646 by Padre Donato da Bomba who wrote a "Relatione Historica".

The description of the Veil at Manoppello is that it is 6.7 x 9.5 inches (17.5 x 24 cm) after having been trimmed in the early 1600's by the Capuchins. There are 26 warp by 26 weft threads in a square centimetre not always at a regular distance from each other. The Veil is white, almost transparent, and is kept on a high altar in a silver monstrance. The fabric is made of a rare silk called Byssus – a precious thread woven from a fine, yellowish flax referred to as "sea silk" and used by ancient Egyptians and Hebrews. It is a kind of fabric found in the graves of the Egyptian Pharaohs.

The Face is displayed in a walnut frame adorned with silver and gold between two pieces of glass. This Manoppello image has two panes of glass with broken chips on bottom which the Vatican archivist Giacomo Grimaldi in 1618 indicated was true of the image that was believed to be in Rome. Also there are dark red features and open eyes and the face is asymmetrical like someone beaten and swollen. The mouth appears slightly open and the eyes are looking upwards.

The case against the Veil's presence in Rome after 1608 stems from some information that Pfeiffer and others have noted:

O   The Veronica that was kept in St. Peter's Basilica in Rome no longer shows any image. Lorenzo Bianchi notes that: "The few scholars of the past who were able to see it close up, such as DeWaal and Wilpert ...saw only a few brown stains. The people who have been able to observe it recently (including Pope John Paul II) found no trace of the image."

O   Pope Paul V (1617) ordered that no reproductions of the Veronica in the 1600's (after the cloth was allegedly stolen in 1608) were to be made unless by a "Canon of St. Peter's." Pfeiffer believes the Pope made this statement because the Veil was stolen. They had no reason to give this order if they were in possession of the Veil in Rome.

O   The eyes on the reproductions of the cloth BEFORE the theft were OPEN. AFTER the theft, the eyes on reproductions of the Veronica are CLOSED. The original Veil showed the eyes open since Jesus was alive at the time Veronica wiped His face.

O   Pope Urban VIII (1623-1644) not only prohibited reproductions of Veronica's veil but also ordered all existing copies to be destroyed. Pfeiffer believes that these orders by Pontiffs of no duplication and destruction of reproductions indicates that the Vatican no longer possessed the original. Further, the Vatican will allow no study of its possession. Vatican custodians have steadfastly refused all requests for any photographs to be taken.

It is interesting to note that Pope Benedict XVI visited Manoppello Sept. 1, 2006 recently after taking his office and prayed before the Image. Some interpret this as a possible concern by the Holy Father that the true image may not in Rome but rather in Manoppello. However sceptics are not convinced. They believe the extremely thin nature of the cloth allowed the image to seep through to be the same on each side. Many believe the similarities between the veil and the Turin Shroud occur because the veil was a deliberate copy of the larger cloth. They also point out the fact that Veronica's meeting with Christ has never been historically documented, and her name itself is a work of fiction – being an amalgamation of the Latin words for 'true image', or 'vera-icon'. The only scientific way of determining the age of the cloth is by carbon dating, but its brittle, delicate state means it could be irreparably damaged during any such tests. For Pfeiffer there is no doubt about the religious authenticity of the veil, and he is entirely convinced that his find is the true artefact.

The Mysterious Painting of Bonaventura Salimbeni

In 1595, Italian artist Bonaventura Salimbeni was commissioned to produce a painting for the right-hand altar of the Church of St. Peter at Montalcino, located within a few miles of Florence. He was a member of a prominent family of artists from nearby Siena, and the goal of his commission was that his work be completed for the Christian Jubilee Year of 1600. According to the message accompanying his signature, Salimbeni's painting was finished right on schedule. What immediately catches the viewer's attention, however, is something pictured in among the Trinity members that to modern eyes seems very familiar, but not from the right time period. The first impression is that it looks exactly like a spheroid satellite with two antennae, something akin to the old Russian sputniks or American vanguard orbiters of the late 1950s. But what is it actually supposed to be?

Ventura di Archangelo Salimbeni (also later called Bevilacqua; 20 January 1568-1613 was an Italian Mannerist painter and printmaker and among the last representatives of a style influenced by the earlier Sienese School of Quattrocento-Renaissance. Salimbeni was born in Siena. He studied painting, together with his half-brother Francesco Vanni, under their father Arcangelo Salimbeni in his native Siena.

At the Basilica della Santissima Annunziata di Firenze, he frescoed lunettes (1605-1608) illustrating events in the history of the Servite Order. In the Duomo di San Salvatore, he executed a magnificent John the Baptist. At about the same time, around 1600, he got an assignment in Assisi for a fresco of the "Resurrection of Christ" and the "Dying Saint Clare is visited by the pope" in the vault of chapel of San Massimo in the Basilica of Santa Maria degli Angeli.

In 1595-1603 Salimbeni got the commission to paint frescoes with scenes from the church's patron saints in the church of Quirico and Giulitta, one of the oldest churches in Siena. As in the church of Santa Trinità, he worked here alongside with the painter Alessandro Casolari. This was a period on non-stop new assignments : three paintings for the church San Lorenzo in San Pietro in Montalcino, the "Donation of the Keys", the "The Glorification of the Eucharist (Disputa of the Eucharist)" and the "Crucifixion". The most famous Montalcino art masterpiece is entitled "The Glorification of the Eucharist," and features a vertical work divided into three segments. The lower third depicts a number of worshipping figures seated before the altar, including priests, cardinals and one individual wearing a papal crown believed to represent Pope Clement VII. The middle third shows the altar itself, and prominently displayed in its centre is the Cup of the Eucharist emblazoned in glowing light. The upper third of the painting symbolizes heaven, dominated by the three Beings of the Holy Trinity who are looking down on the earthly scene below and giving their blessings – God the Father depicted as a Moses-like bearded old man, God the Son as Jesus Christ, and the Holy Spirit portrayed as a Dove hovering above the centre. While the trinity members is holding each of the antennae with one of their hand. The antennae itself is attached into a sphere object.

Renaissance art experts interpret the strange sphere as representing the universe, showing the faint lines of celestial longitude and latitude, plus the images of an obscure sun and an exaggerated crescent moon shining from inside. The two "antennae" – one held by God

24

the Father and the other by God the Son – are said to be "scepters" symbolizing divine rulership. But the closer one examines the object, the more inconsistencies arise with this somewhat limited interpretation. If the "sphere" is supposed to be the universe, why are there no stars or constellations depicted shining from inside it? In fact, there is nothing transparent about it – the sphere on the contrary appears to be solid, with what looks like a metallic sheen reflected off its exterior. The so-called celestial "lines" more realistically suggest the seams of metal plating that covers the outer circumference, made of a strange blue-black material.

The "sun" is too indistinct to represent the solar body, and in a technological context more likely is an electrical light source designed to illuminate the sphere's immediate surroundings. As for the "moon," its unnatural double crescent with touching ends was not meant to depict a flat circle in two dimensions, but forms the edge of a three-dimensional narrow-width cylinder seen from an angle – what we today would identify as a camera lens protruding off the sphere's surface.

Without a doubt the most outlandish features are the two "antennae". They bear no resemblance whatsoever to any type of "scepter" or staff of power used by Renaissance officials, political or religious. Usually a scepter is pointed at the bottom end and has some symbol or figure prominently displayed at its apex. In contrast, the two objects held by the Trinity members are slightly wider at their bases than their tops. In fact, on much closer inspection, it can be clearly seen that both objects have an inherent "telescoping" design. They are segmented into distinct sections which could be collapsed into a smaller size, and when pulled apart would extend to greater lengths. The problem is, "telescoping" was a mechanical innovation which was not invented until the early eighteenth century. What is it doing being portrayed in a painting over a hundred years too soon? Even stranger, it can be observed that the two antennae are fastened to the sphere with gold or brass-coloured grommet-rings, and certain lengths of the antennae also have grommet-rings. A grommet-ring is a threaded eyelet that is used to tighten and hold metal segments in place. Once again, we are dealing with something from another time, for such an innovation did not appear in industrial machinery design until the mid-nineteenth century.

And then there is the anomaly of the antennae themselves. The existence of antennae for the earliest radio transmissions did not appear until the first part of the twentieth century. Going a step beyond, it can also be noticed that the sphere is clearly depicted as not resting on the background cloud it is pictured with, or sits on any surface whatsoever, but is hovering in place, held up by the "invisible powers" of the Trinity. Also, the sphere casts no well-defined shadow, which means that it did not appear in the physical but was more likely seen as a projected image.

Ufologists and "ancient astronaut" theorists have been quick to seize upon this out-of-place object as being proof of an extraterrestrial visitation, possibly a spaceship seen by the artist. The problem is, there is nothing especially "alien" about this device. In fact, every one of its aspects is recognizable as the product of a purely earth-bound technology. The real mystery is not one of place but one of time. The sudden appearance of something displaying elements of a futuristic technology in the sixteenth century strongly suggests that this is ultimately where it must have come from, the future. Either that, or it was a projection far forward from a lost advanced civilization long disappeared that developed along technological lines not that much different from our own today.

The questions remain, what exactly did the artist see, and why did he portray it in the manner shown in his painting? Undoubtedly, Salimbeni regarded his encounter as a God-given vision, and through his artistry sought to comprehend it in that context. The device could have suddenly and unexpectedly appeared before him as if out of thin air, then quickly vanished after only a few seconds. But having an artistic eye sensitive to details, he very likely immediately made sketches of what he saw so he could later better remember it and portray it in the larger and more permanent masterpiece work we see today.

St. Prest Fossils

In April of 1863, Jules Desnoyers, of the French National Museum, came to St. Prest, in northwestern France, to gather fossils. From the sandy gravels, he recovered part of a rhinoceros tibia. He noticed on the bone a series of narrow grooves. He also observed small circular marks that could well have been made by a pointed implement. To Desnoyers, some of the grooves appeared to have been produced by a sharp knife or blade of flint. If Desnoyers concluded correctly that the marks on many of the bones had been made by flint implements, then it would appear that human beings had been present in France during Pliocene era. It is believed that at the end of the Pliocene, about 2 million years ago, the modern human species had not yet come into being.

Jules Pierre François Stanislaus Desnoyers (October 8, 1800 – 1887) was a French geologist and archaeologist. Desnoyers was born at Nogent-le-Rotrou, in the department of Eure-et-Loir. Becoming interested in geology at an early age, he was one of the founders of the Geological Society of France in 1830.

In 1863, Desnoyers examined his collections of St. Prest fossils at the museums of Chartres and the School of Mines in Paris and saw they bore the same types of marks. He then reported his findings to the French Academy of Sciences. Some modern scientists have said that the St. Prest site belongs to the Late

Pliocene. The presence at that time in Europe of beings using stone tools in a sophisticated manner would seem almost impossible. Only in Africa should one find primitive human ancestors, and these were limited to Australopithecus and Homo habilis, the latter considered the first toolmaker. According to reports by other scientists, the St. Prest site might be more recent than the Pliocene – perhaps as little as 1.2-1.6 million years old. But the incised bones would still be anomalous. Even in the nineteenth century, Desnoyers's discoveries of incised bones at St. Prest provoked controversy. Opponents argued that the marks were made by the tools of the workmen who excavated them. But Desnoyers showed that the cut marks were covered with mineral deposits just like the other surfaces of the fossil bones.

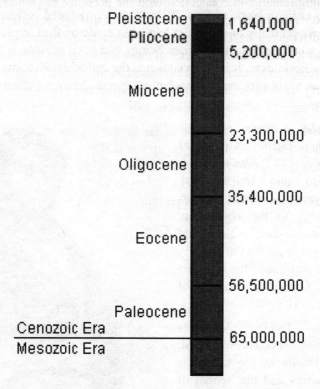

Pleistocene
Pliocene   1,640,000

    5,200,000

Miocene

    23,300,000

Oligocene

    35,400,000

Eocene

    56,500,000

Paleocene
Cenozoic Era
Mesozoic Era   65,000,000

The prominent British geologist Sir Charles Lyell suggested the marks were made by rodents' teeth, but French prehistorian Gabriel de Mortillet said the marks could not have been made by animals. He instead suggested that they were made by sharp stones moved by

28

geological pressure across the bones. Louis Bourgeois, a clergyman who had also earned a reputation as a distinguished paleontologist, carefully searched the strata at St. Prest for such evidence. By his patient research he eventually found a number of flints that he believed were genuine tools and made them the subject of a report to the Academy of Sciences in January, 1867.

The famous French anthropologist Armand de Quatrefages said the tools included scrapers, borers, and lance points. Even this did not satisfy de Mortillet, who said the flints discovered by Bourgeois at St. Prest had been chipped by geological pressure. In 1910, the famous American paleontologist Henry Fairfield Osborn made these interesting remarks in connection with the presence of stone tools at St. Prest: "the earliest traces of man in beds of this age were the incised bones discovered by Desnoyers at St. Prest near Chartres in 1863. Doubt as to the artificial character of these incisions has been removed by the recent explorations of Laville and Rutot, which resulted in the discovery of eolithic flints, fully confirming the discoveries of the Abbé Bourgeois in these deposits in 1867."

Michael Cremo said, "So as far as the discoveries at St. Prest are concerned, it should now be apparent that we are dealing with paleontological problems that cannot be quickly or easily resolved. Certainly, there is not sufficient reason to categorically reject these bones as evidence for a human presence in the Pliocene."

Reck's Skeleton Mystery

Olduvai Gorge in the East African nation of Tanzania is one of the most famous archaeological sites in the world. It is especially renowned as the place where Louis Leakey discovered fossils of a variety of apemen, including *Homo habilis*. They are mentioned in most textbooks. But these textbooks are usually silent about the very first skeleton discovered at Olduvai Gorge, called the Reck's skeleton that was found in Upper Bed II which dating from 1,15 million years old. George Grant MacCurdy a leading anthropologist from Yale University, considered Reck's skeleton to be genuine. According to today's orthodox scientific opinion, humans like us did not come into existence until about 100,000 years old. In 1913, a German scientist, Hans Reck, came to Olduvai Gorge to search for fossils. One of Reck's African collectors saw a bone protruding from the earth and started to excavate. Reck came and completed the excavation. Using hammers and chisels, workers under Reck's direction took out an almost complete, anatomically modern, human skeleton in a solid block of hardened sedimentary rock.

Homo eragaster OH 9   Pranthropus boisei OH 5   Homo habilis OH 62   Homo habilis OH 048

Reck identified a sequence of five beds at Olduvai Gorge. The skeleton was from the upper part of Bed II. At Reck's site, the overlying layers (Beds III, IV, and V) had been worn away by erosion.

According to modern dating methods, Bed II is from 1.15 million to 1.7 million years old. Reck carefully studied the geology of the site, and concluded, "The bed in which the human remains were found... showed no signs of disturbance. The spot appeared exactly like any other in the horizon. There was no evidence of any refilled hole or grave". So this skeleton is evidence that anatomically modern humans were existing in the very distant past, over one million years ago. Reck returned to Germany, taking the skeleton's skull with him personally, while the block of rock containing the rest of the skeleton followed by ship. When his first reports on the skeleton came out, he won the support of many scientists, including the American anthropologist George Grant MacCurdy of Yale University. The skeleton bore the same relation to the stratified beds as did the other mammalian remains, and was dug out of the hard clay tufa with hammer and chisel just as these were. In other words, the conditions of the find were such as to exclude the possibility of an interment. The human bones are therefore as old as the deposit." Mac Curdy also agreed that the skeleton was of modern type and not like an earlier form of human such as the Neandertals.

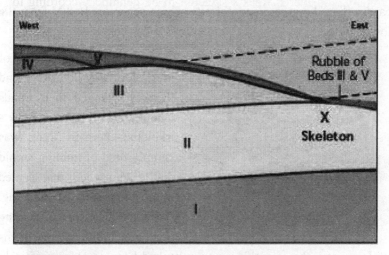

Other scientists, including Louis Leakey, disagreed that the skeleton was as old as Bed II. To settle the question, Leakey and some others went to Olduvai Gorge to personally examine the site in 1931. After careful study, Leakey concluded that Reck had been right. Reck and Leakey, along with A. T. Hopwood of the British Museum of Natural History, published a report in Nature (1931, vol. 128, p. 724) affirming that the skeleton was as old as the bed in which it had been found, Bed II. Other scientists continued to object to the great age of Reck's skeleton.

Reck and Leakey held their ground, until in 1932 an English geologist named P. G. H. Boswell published in Nature (vol. 130, pp. 237-238) a report in which he claimed he had found reddish pebbles from Bed III and white calcrete fragments from Bed V in a sample of the matrix from which Reck's skeleton had been extracted. The sample that Boswell studied had been sent to him from Munich. And there is no way of knowing if it came from the matrix that directly encased the skeleton or from some other sediments that had come in the crate along with the skeleton.

Nevertheless, both Reck and Leakey joined Boswell, Hopwood, and Solomon concluding in a report published in Nature (1933, vol. 131, pp. 397-398) that "it seems highly probable that the skeleton was intrusive into Bed II and that the date of the intrusion is not earlier than the great unconformity which separates Bed V from the lower series."

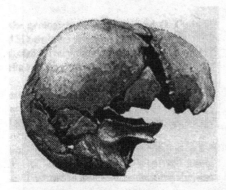

It remains somewhat of a mystery why both Reck and Leakey changed their minds about a Bed II date for Reck's skeleton. Perhaps Reck was simply tired of fighting an old battle against odds that seemed more and more overwhelming. With the discovery of Beijing man and additional specimens of Java man, the scientific community had become more uniformly committed to the idea that a transitional ape-man was the only proper inhabitant of the Middle Pleistocene. An anatomically modern Homo sapiens skeleton in Bed II of Olduvai Gorge did not make sense except as a fairly recent burial. This would still give the anatomically modern human skeleton an age of perhaps as much as 400,000 years, because the oldest part of Bed V is about that old. And 400,000 years is still far beyond the orthodox scientific estimates for the maximum age of anatomically modern humans. Unfortunately, during World War II, Reck's skeleton, except for the skull, vanished from the Munich Museum.

Reck excavated the skeleton from Bed II in Olduvai Gorge. He carefully searched for signs of intrusive burial (especially materials from Bed III and higher levels) and found none. Louis Leakey and other scientists, who personally studied the skeleton in Germany and investigated the Olduvai Gorge site itself, confirmed Reck's reports. So probably the sample examined by Boswell was not from the actual matrix of the skeleton. It was from other materials that came in the box with the skeleton from Africa. The most reasonable conclusion: "Reck's skeleton is evidence for the existence of anatomically modern humans over one million years ago."

Tecaxic Calixtlahuaca Head

The Tecaxic-Calixtlahuaca head is a terracotta head, probably originally part of a larger figurine, discovered in 1933 among pre-Columbian grave goods in the Tecaxic-Calixtlahuaca zone in the Toluca Valley, approximately 65 kilometres west of Mexico City. Because of the head's non-Amerind facial features, including a beard, and its unusual style, some believe that it is of Roman origin, and thus evidence of pre-Columbian trans-oceanic contact. The site where the head was found seems to be a genuine pre-colonial site undisturbed during the colonial period. A thermoluminescence test performed in 1995 by P.Schaaf and G.A.Wagner in the FS Archaeömetrie unit in Heidelberg, Germany, established its age limits between the 9th century B.C. and the middle of the 13th century A.D, confirming that it is a pre-colonial artefact. Bernard Andreae of the German Institute of Archaeology in Rome, Italy, confirmed the style as Roman and proposed the 2nd century A.D as datation, based on the hairstyle and the beard.

✿❦69❦✿

The Piri Rei's Map

Captain Arlington H. Mallery was puzzled. The captain was retired from the U.S. Navy and made examining old maps his hobby. The image of the map he had in front of him at first had only seemed mildly interesting. It had been commissioned by a Turkish Admiral named Piri Ibn Haji Memmed in 1513. The map had drawn the attention of scholars in 1929 when it had been discovered in the archives of the Imperial Palace in Constantinople.

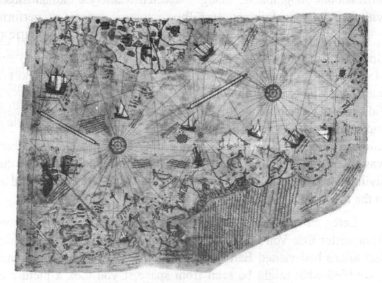

The map showed the outline of South America very accurately. This was surprising since Columbus had discovered the New World only 21 years earlier in 1492. Notes made by Piri indicated he had based his map on earlier maps, including one consulted by Columbus before his famous voyage. This excited the scholars since there had been rumours that there existed a pre-Columbian map of the New World. Piri's claim that he had possessed the "lost map" intrigued historians.

It wasn't the accuracy of the South American coastline that interested Mallery, though. It was what was shown at the very bottom of the map: a chunk of land that looked very much like Antarctica. This was surprising since Antarctica had not been discovered until 1820. Even more intriguing was a section of the coastline of this southern continent. Part of it looked very much like the coast of Queen Maud Land which was a section of Antarctica. The strange thing was that the coast of Queen Maud Land had been covered with a thick sheet of ice for many centuries and its shape was only known now to modern mapmakers through the use of modern seismographic equipment.

This made Mallory wonder if the Admiral had somehow owned maps that dated back before the ice sheet covered the coast and if the coast had been somehow surveyed from the air. Most serious professional geographers, though, rejected Mallery's radical theory without even considering it carefully.

Professor Charles H. Hapgood, of Keene State College at the University of New Hampshire, did take an interest in the map and Mallory's thoughts. Professor Hapgood was known for his support of unorthodox theories. With the help of some of his students, Hapgood did a careful examination of Piri's map and several other old maps and published a book on the subject called *Maps of the Ancient Sea Kings*. The book suggests that at one time in the ancient past there was a world-wide civilization with advanced technology. Though this civilization was destroyed, some of its knowledge survived to wind up in the maps.

Later, an even more radical theory for Piri's map was advanced from writer Eric Von Daniken. Von Daniken, a supporter of the idea that aliens had visited Earth in the distant past, noted that the map resembled what might be seen from space if you took a picture of Earth from directly over Cairo, Egypt. He suggested that the map was the result of aerial photographs taken from an alien spaceship.

Critics of Hapgood and Von Daniken offer a more mundane explanation for the map. They start by pointing out that lots of maps from that era displayed a continent at the bottom of the Earth, though none had yet been found. There was a general belief going back to the time of the Greeks that all the continents must have been connected at one time. This lead to the belief in a southern continent (Interestingly enough, they were correct. The modern theory of plate tectonics supports the idea of single land mass in the very distant past).

The critics point out that the land mass shown on the map may have a similar coastline to that of Queen Maud Land, but the similarity is not unmistakable. What is on Piri's map, they argue, is just a lucky attempt to display an unknown, but suspected land. The similarity, say critics, is just coincidence. They also point out that the map shows South America and Antarctica connected, which they have not been for many millions of years. Also information about weather conditions and animal life in Antarctica as found on the map is completely wrong.

Other experts speculate that though the first recorded sighting of land in the Antarctica was in 1820, there may have been earlier unreported voyages to the southern reaches. Though this might not explain the coastline of Queen Maud Land on the Piri map, it might be the reason that there was such a strong belief in the existence of a southern continent.

So is the map proof of lost civilizations or aliens? Probably not by itself. Still, it is another piece of the puzzle of mankind's history that does not quite seem to fit.

The Unsolved Mystery
of Phaistos Disc

The Phaistos Disc (also spelled Phaistos Disk, Phaestos Disc) is a disk of fired clay from the Minoan palace of Phaistos, possibly dating to the middle or late Minoan Bronze Age (2nd millennium BC). It is about 15 cm (5.9 in) in diametre and covered on both sides with a spiral of stamped symbols. Its purpose and meaning, and even its original geographical place of manufacture, remain disputed, making it one of the most famous mysteries of archaeology. This unique object is now on display at the archaeological museum of Heraklion in Crete, Greece. The undeciphered Phaistos Disc is one of the greatest puzzles in archaeology. Almost everything about this ancient artefact is controversial, from its purpose and meaning to its original area of manufacture. The mysterious clay tablet was found on the Greek island of Crete, at the Minoan Palace site at Phaistos. But who made it, and what was it used for?

The Phaistos Disc captured the imagination of amateur and professional archeologists, and many attempts have been made to decipher the code behind the disc's signs. While most linguistic interpretations assume a syllabary, others would only consider alphabetic and purely logographical interpretations. Scholarly attempts at decipherment are thought to be unlikely to succeed unless more examples of the signs turn up somewhere, as it is generally thought that there is not enough context available for meaningful analysis. Although the Phaistos Disc is generally accepted as authentic by archaeologists, a few scholars have forwarded the opinion that the disc is a forgery or a hoax.

The disc was discovered in 1908 by the Italian archaeologist Luigi Pernier in the Minoan palace-site of Phaistos, on the south coast of Crete. The sophisticated Bronze Age civilization of the Minoans reached its height in the period c.1700 B.C., and began to decline about three centuries later, when many of their palaces were destroyed. The archaeologists came upon the strange object in a basement room in the northeast apartments of the palace, together with a clay tablet inscribed in Linear A (an undeciphered script used on Crete until around 1450 B.C.), and pieces of neopalatial pottery (c. 1700 B.C. – 1600 B.C.). The palace had collapsed during an earthquake, which has been linked by some researchers to the massive volcanic eruption on the nearby Aegean island of Thera (modern day Santorini) c. 1628 B.C. the precise age of the Phaistos disc is disputed; the archaeological context of the find suggests a date not later than 1700 B.C., though the modern opinion is that it could have been created as late as 1650 B.C.

The enigmatic disc is made of baked clay with an average diametre of 6.2 inches, and a thickness of 0.8 inches. Both sides of the disc are covered with a hieroglyphic inscription arranged in a spiral. The inscription was made by impressing wood or ivory hieroglyphic seals or stamps into the wet clay, and then baking the clay at a high temperature to harden it. It has been noted that occasionally on the artefact, a symbol slightly overlaps the one to its right, which demonstrates that the creator was stamping towards the left, that resulted in the text spiralling inwards to the centre. The Phaistos Disc represents what is, in effect, the earliest form of printing anywhere in the world. Printed into the disc are a total of 242 individual impressions divided into 61 groups by vertical lines; there are 45 different signs, including depictions of running men, heads with feather crowns, women, children, animals, birds, insects, tools, weapons, and plants.

One or two of these symbols have been identified as vaguely similar to the Cretan hierogyphs in use during the early to mid-second millennium B.C.

What is so puzzling about the artefact is why the Minoans were using a primitive pictographic language at the same time as Linear A, a much more advanced script. Perhaps the primitive nature of the script on the disc points to a much earlier date for the object than is presently accepted. However, this is not necessarily the case, as archaic forms of writing often survive into much later periods, usually in the form of sacred or religious texts, as was the case in ancient Egypt. Furthermore, the text on the Phaistos Disc is unique; no other examples of the script stamped on it have ever been located. This uniqueness, and the fact that the text is fairly brief, makes it extremely difficult to translate even a small part of it. That the inscription was made using a set of stamps would imply that there was a large-scale production of objects impressed with this script, which, for one reason or another, have not yet surfaced in archaeological investigations.

A difficulty with understanding the artefact is that no one knows exactly how the symbols on it are meant to be interpreted. Does the disc contain a hieroglyphic inscription, or are the pictograms meant to be taken at face value? Although some image on the Phaistos Disc are pictures of familiar objects, trying to understand these literally does not help with obtaining any coherent meaning from the disc. Many linguists believe the text is a series of written signs representing syllables (known as syllabary), while others assume it is a syllabary combined with pictorial symbols used to express a concept or idea (known as ideograms). The combination of a syllabary and ideograms would make it comparable to all known syllabaries of Greece and the ancient Near East, including Minoan Linear B script, hieroglyphic writing, and the cuneiform. (The latter consists of pictograms drawn on clay tablets with a pen made from a sharpened reed, and originated in ancient Sumeria in the late-fourth millennium B.C.)

The Palette of Narmer is an interesting example of such texts. It was discovered in Nekhen (modern Hierakonpolis), the ancient pre-dynastic capital of Egypt, by English archaeologist James E. Quibell, in 1894. It dates roughly to 3200 B.C. and includes some of the earliest hieroglyphic inscriptions ever discovered. The palette of narmer uses combination of hieroglyphs and pictographic symbols, which are to be taken literally to mean what they depict, indicating a possible parallel with the Phaistos Disc, in the sense that it could be interpreted as containing a mixture of ancient Cretan hieroglyphs and pictographs.

The tremendous difficulty of translation without further examples of the script has not dissuaded both scholars and amateurs from attempting the task. In fact, the unique nature of the text has added to its mystique and enthralled rather than repelled investigators. The distinctiveness of the disc has, unfortunately, meant that there have been a number of highly imaginative and unsubstantiated translations and interpretations of the text. Perhaps the most extreme among them is that the object contains a message left thousand years ago by extraterrestrial visitors, or an ancient Antlantean civilization, for future generations to discover. The question of what exactly the message contains or why it was written in such a primitive script by supposedly advanced aliens (or Atlanteans) has, of course, never been answered.

Over the last 100 years numerous attempts have been made to try and identify the language on the disc. In 1975, Jean Faucounau published a translation, maintaining that the language was a pre-Greek, syllabic writing of a culture he identifies as Proto-Ionians, a people with closer ties to ancient troy than to Crete. According to Faucounau's decipherment, the Phaistos Disc described the career and funeral of a Proto-Ionian king named Arion. His translation has, however, not been accepted as sound by most scholars on the subject.

In 2000, Greek author Efi Polygiannakis published (in Greek) a book entitled *The Disc Speaks in Greek*, claiming that the inscription on the disc was written in the syllabic writing system of an ancient Greek dialect. Dr. Steven Fischer's Evidence of Hellenic Dialect in the Phaistos Disk (1988) also identifies the text as syllabic writing in a Greek dialect. One clue to the meaning of the object is the context in which it was found. The fact that the Phaistos Disc was unearthed in an underground temple depository has persuade some researchers of its religious significance, suggesting that the text was possibly a sacred hymn or ritual. Several image groups in the text are repeated, which would suggest a refrain, and perhaps each side of the disc represents a verse from a song, hymn, or ritual incantation. In fact, Sir Arthur Evans, excavator of

Knossos (the ceremonial and political centre of Minoan civilization), concluded that the disc contained part of the text of a sacred song.

The original discoverer of the disc, Italian archaeologist Luigi Pernier, also believed it had ritual significance. Nevertheless, though the Phaistos Disc was found at a Minoan palace site, there is no absolute proof that it originated on Crete at all. It may have been imported from just about anywhere in the Mediterranean, or even from the Near East. Not a single example of the stamped or printed method of writing on the Phaistos Disc has been found in the numerous excavations carried out on Crete over the past 100 years. This complete lack of comparative material has suggested to some that this disc is a forgery. A thermoluminescence dating test would certainly prove whether the object was made during the last hundred years, or if it did in fact date to the Minoan period.

So far the Greek authorities have been unwilling to submit the disc to such a test. Consequently, the possibility that the object is a forgery made in the early 1900s – using the limited knowledge of the Minoan culture available at the time – is perhaps a far-fetched, but by no means out of the question scenario. In connection with the hoax theory, an intriguing find was made in 1992 in the basement of a house in Vladikavkaz, Russia. This was a fragment of a clay disc, smaller in size than the Phaistos Disc, but apparently a copy of it, though the symbols on this disc were incised rather than stamped.

There were rumours of a hoax, but the Russian disc mysteriously disappeared a few years later, and nothing has been heard since. Despite the apparent thanklessness of the task, many researchers throughout the world still work diligently attempting to decipher the disc. But the extreme variations in the many purported translations have made scholars doubtful of any future success at decipherment, and indicate to many that while it remains an isolated example of its kind, the disc can never be properly understood. We can only hope that future archaeological excavations in Crete, or perhaps elsewhere in the Mediterranean, will turn up further examples of this mysterious script. Until then, the Phaistos Disc, now on display in the archaeological museum of Heraklion in Crete, will remain a unique enigma.

Nomoli Statues

The Nomoli Statues is the small figure of stone that has been found by local people when searching for diamonds in Sierra Leone, West Africa. This statues is the most unusual, outstanding and oldest Nomoli artefact. The age is estimated of 17000 years. When it was found a certain noise was recognized when it was moved. A sculptor cut out one piece of the object. He discovered a hole and also a very small ball of metal. So where do those mysterious stone figures come from? Are they relics of a foreign and sunken culture? Did the unknown creator have had a profound purpose? Scientists, especially ethnologists, developed numerous theories about those figures. They do not have the same opinion because the origin and the purpose of the sculptures are unexplained.

Myth and legend of Western Africa says that in ancient times a people of angels lived in heaven. As a cause of bad behaviour God banned them from the divine empire. To punish the angels he transformed them into men and sends them to Earth. The Nomoli Statues are said to be a reminder of those once divine creatures. The faces of the Nomoli figures show typical characteristics: The statues are made of different sorts of stone, soft materials as well as hard granite. They have a very big nose like an eagle with nostrils, a big mouth, sometimes showing teeth and significant eyes. Their skulls are flat. The objects were about 40cm tall; their origin is unknown. The dating of the Nomoli still is a problem. According to the geological stratums in which they were found, they must be 2500 to 17000 years old. The figures that laid in deeper stratums were raw and simple made. The sculptures have various poses and expression. The majority are human figures, some riding on horses, most of them sitting with crossed legs or on their knees. Some put their faces in their hands. Sometimes the figures have weapons or a shield.

The natives often call the figures "men in stone". But some see them as guardian god and god who brings luck and they put them on their fields to guard and increase the harvest. Some native tribes like the Mande and Kissi in Guinea put such statues of Nomolis on their fields. So a "vegetation cult" developed that is seen in connection with death. They put the stones on their fields and made them sacrifices if the harvest was rich. If harvest was bad the Nomoli have been punished ritually and whipped.

Angelo Pitoni, an Italian geologist, deals with the Nomoli statues. He took some organic samples from the places the figures where found. To define the age different materials have been taken, e.g. founds made of wood (a stick that was found in a depth of 10 metres). Prof. Giorgio Belluomini from University of Rome also examined the artefact and estimated its age of 400 to 500 years. In 1992 the object was analysed three times and the C-14-dating showed an age of 2470 years, +/- 50 years. Until that day one thought that the only civilization in Western

Africa was the so-called Afro-Portuguese civilization, about 400 years old. But the Nomoli objects do not fit this conception.

Also there is some mysterious stones that are connected with the strange Nomoli figures called the "Sky Stones". They were also found in Sierra Leone in a great quantity. Based on local legend, it says that the part of the sky the Nomoli lived in turned into stone. Then it split and fell down on earth in huge pieces of rock. The stars that were in this part of the sky have also been destroyed and rests came to earth. Sparkling rests of those stars are the diamonds.

Natives showed excavation-places where in a depth of 40 m to 40 cm numerous blue stones were found. They had different sizes. Their colour, similar to Cobalt, some pieces have been analysed in different laboratories in the whole world. The results based on analysis made by the Institute for Precious Stones of the Museum of Natural History have been astonishing: It showed that the stones were made artificially, the pulverised samples consist of 77% oxygen, 20% carbon and lime, silicon and traces of iridium. However, there is no iridium on Earth, unless it was brought in from space by a meteorite.

Neolithic Tools from the California Gold Mine

In the middle of the nineteenth century, miners discovered hundreds of stone artefacts and human skeletons deep inside their tunnels at Table Mountain and other locations in the gold mining region. These bones and artefacts were found embedded in formations that geologists now say belong to the Eocene period (38-55 million years). This evidence was reported to the scientific world by Dr. J. D. Whitney, the chief government geologist of California, in his book *The Auriferous Gravels of the Sierra Nevada of California*, published by Harvard University's Peabody Museum of Comparative Zoology in 1880. But the evidence was dropped from scientific discourse because it contradicted with the current Darwinist explanations of human origins.

In 1849, gold was discovered in the gravels of ancient riverbeds on the slopes of the Sierra Nevada Mountains in central

California, drawing hordes of rowdy adventurers to places like Brandy City, Last Chance, Lost Camp, You Bet, and Poker Flat. At first, solitary miners panned for flakes and nuggets in the gravels that had found their way into the present streambeds. But soon gold-mining companies brought more extensive resources into play, some sinking shafts into mountainsides, following the gravel deposits wherever they led, while others washed the auriferous (gold-bearing) gravels from hillsides with high-pressure jets of water. The miners found hundreds of stone artefacts, and, more rarely, human fossils. The most significant artefacts were reported to the scientific community by Dr. J. D. Whitney.

The artefacts from surface deposits and hydraulic mining were of doubtful age, but the artefacts from deep mine shafts and tunnels could be more securely dated. J. D. Whitney thought the geological evidence indicated the auriferous gravels were at least Pliocene in age. But modern geologists think some of the gravel deposits are from the Eocene. Many shafts were sunk at Table Mountain in Tuolumne County, going under thick layers of a basaltic volcanic material called latite before reaching the gold-bearing gravels. In some cases, the shafts extended horizontally for hundreds of feet beneath the latite cap. Discoveries from the gravels just above the bedrock could be from 33.2 to 55 million years old, but discoveries from other gravels may be anywhere from 9 to 55 million years old.

William B. Holmes, a physical anthropologist at the Smithsonian Institution, said, "If Professor Whitney had fully appreciated the story of human evolution as it is understood today, he would have hesitated to announce the conclusions formulated, notwithstanding the imposing array of testimony with which he was confronted." In other words, if the evidence did not fit the theory, then the evidence had to be set aside, which is exactly what happened. Today, some of the artefacts mentioned by Whitney are still in the Phoebe Hearst Museum of Anthropology at the University of California at Berkeley.

Darwinism and other isms also influenced the treatment of archaeological evidence at Hueyatlaco, Mexico. In the 1970s, archaeologists led by Cynthia Irwin-Williams found stone tools associated with butchered animal bones in excavations there. A team of geologists, including Virginia Steen-McIntyre, came in to date the site. Using four different methods (uranium series dates on butchered animal bone, zircon fission track dating on volcanic layers above the artefact layers, tephra hydration dating of volcanic crystals found in the volcanic layers above the artefact layers, and standard stratigraphic analysis), the geologists determined the age of the site was at least 250,000 years.

The archaeologists refused to accept an age this great for the site, because: (1) they believed no human beings capable of making such artefacts existed 250,000 years ago anywhere in the world and (2) they believed no human beings entered North America until about 15,000 or 20,000 years ago, maximum.

Nebra Sky Disc

The Nebra Sky Disc is one of the most fascinating, and some
would say controversial, archaeological finds of recent years. Dated
to 1600 B.C., this bronze disc has a diametre of 32 cm and weighs
around 4 pounds. It is patinated blue-green and embossed with gold
leaf symbols, which appear to represent a crescent moon, the sun
(or perhaps a full moon), stars, a curved gold band on the edge of
the disc (which probably represent one of the horizons) These are
interpreted generally as a sun or full moon, a lunar crescent, and stars
(including a cluster interpreted as the Pleiades). Two golden arcs along
the sides, marking the angle between the solstices, were added later. A
final addition was another arc at the bottom surrounded with multiple
strokes (of uncertain meaning, variously interpreted as a Solar Barge
with numerous oars, as the Milky Way or as a rainbow). Another gold
band on the opposite side is missing.

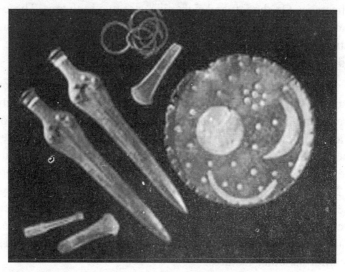

The disk is attributed to a site near Nebra, Saxony-Anhalt in
Germany. It has been associated with the Bronze Age Unetice culture.

The disk is unlike any known artistic style from the period, and had initially been suspected of being a forgery, but is now widely accepted as authentic.

The disc was found in a cache of bronze goods, including axes and daggers, in a Bronze Age site at the top of a mountain, the Mittelberg. It is thought that the site would originally have had a good view of the skies and the horizon all around, and might have been used as an observatory. The astronomical information on the disc is particular to the latitude of the location where it was found, so it is likely that the disc was made for and used in the site where it was finally hidden.

Description and Interpretation of the Symbols on the Disc

At one edge of the disc is an arc which looks like a boat sailing on the sea. The tiny indentations along each side of the arc may represent the oars of the ship.

Many ancient peoples imagined the sun as travelling from Western to Eastern horizon after it set in a special ship. This may be a depiction of the Ship of the Sun. If so, it means that the disc should be held in a vertical plane, with this 'boat' at the bottom. In this orientation, the rest of the symbols in the centre of the disc fall into place as a picture of the heavens. On the left and right sides are two long arcs. These span about 80 degrees each. The difference between sunrise on the summer solstice and on the winter solstice is 82.7 degrees at this latitude, as is the difference between the sunsets on the two solstices.

The two arcs are said to represent the portions of the horizon where the sun rises during the year. (The gold coating on the left arc, representing sunset, has fallen off and is lost). Between the two arcs are a full circle and a crescent. The crescent obviously represents a crescent moon, while the large circle may be the sun or a full moon. (The gold on the sun/full moon circle is damaged). In the background are 23 stars dotted in an apparently random pattern, and one group of seven stars which is said to represent the Pleiades star cluster (the Seven Sisters or M45). X-Rays indicate that under the gold of the right arc are two more stars, so it is likely that the two arcs were added some time after the other features.

Intrigued by the possibility of the Nebra Disc as an astronomical device, Professor Wolfhard Schloesser of the University of Bochum measured the angle between the pair of arcs on either side of the disc, and found that it was 82 degrees. Fascinatingly, at Mittelberg hill, between the high mid-summer sunset and the low mid-summer sunset, the sun appears to travel around 82 degrees along the horizon. This angle would vary from place to place. Schloesser concluded that the pair of arcs along the circumference of the Nebra Disc did indeed depict the sun solstices accurately for its location. This would suggest that the Bronze Age agricultural societies of central Europe made sophisticated celestial measurements far earlier than has been suspected.

It is an astronomical fact that when the crescent moon appears in a particular orientation to the Pleiades, there is an eclipse seven days later. Is the picture on the disc intended to portray this? We'll never know for sure, as there is not enough detail in the picture. Around the outside of the disc is a ring of crude holes punched through the metal. It is thought that these are for attaching the disc to something, rather than forming part of the astronomical diagram. Perhaps the disc was stitched to a piece of heavy cloth?

What was the Purpose of the Disc?

If the disc was intended as an astronomical tool, the only thing on it that is accurate is the pair of arcs. With the disc in a horizontal plane, these could be used to examine the position of sunrise and sunset; the cache site was on the top of a hill, a good place for looking at the sun. The site was surrounded by an artificial low bank, which could be used for measuring the position of the sun on the horizon. The position of the sun at sunrise and sunset is a good indication of the time of year and can be used to predict times for planting and harvesting crops; the Bronze Age people were an agricultural society. Alternatively, the disc might have been a teaching tool, explaining the mysteries of the night sky to students.

In late 2004, the Nebra Disc became enmeshed in controversy. German archaeologist Professor Peter Schauer, of Regensbury University, claimed that the disc was a modern fake, and any idea that it was a Bronze Age map of the heavens was "a piece of fantasy." Professor Schauer stated that the supposedly Bronze Age patina on the artefact had been artificially created in a workshop "using acid, urine, and a blowtorch" and was not ancient at all. The holes around the edge of the disc, he insisted, were too perfect to be ancient, and must have been made by a relatively modern machine.

His own conclusion was that the object was a 19th century Siberian Shaman's drum. However, it later emerged that Schauer had never studied the artefact himself prior to making his claim, nor did he publish any of his theories in a peer-reviewed journal. But Shcauer's objections still shocked the German archaeological community and raised some important questions about the authenticity of the disc. The first was that, because of the circumstances of its discovery, the Nebra Disc had no secure archaeological context. Thus, it was extremely difficult to date accurately, especially as there was nothing similar with which to compare it.

The dating was done on the object depended upon the typological dating of the Bronze Age weapons that had been offered for sale with it, and were supposed to be from the same site. These axes and swords were dated to the middle of the second millennium B.C. Solid evidence for the antiquity of the disc was provided by the Halle institute for Archaeological research in Germany. The Institute submitted the artefact to an exhaustive series of tests that confirm its authenticity. For example, the copper used on the disc has been traced to a Bronze Age mine in the Austrian Alps.

Tests also discovered that a practically unique mixture of hard crystal malachite covers the artefact. In addition to this, microphotography of the corrosion on the disc has also produced images that proved that it was a genuinely ancient artefact, and could not be have been produced as a fake.

The latest examinations of the disc, by a group of German scholars in early 2006, came to the conclusion that it was indeed genuine, and had functioned as a complex astronomical clock for the synchronization of solar and lunar calendars. The Nebra Sky Disc is thus the earliest known guide to the heavens, and certainly, along with the site, the first examples of the detailed astronomical knowledge in Europe. But perhaps that is not the end of the stories. Wolfhard Schlosser believes intriguingly, that the disc (currently valued at $11.2 million) was one of a pair, and that the other is still out there waiting to be found.

Narmer Palette

The Narmer Palette, with a height of 64 cm and a width of 42 cm, also known as the Great Hierakonpolis Palette or the Palette of Narmer, is a significant Egyptian archeological find, dating from about the 31st century BC, containing some of the earliest hieroglyphic inscriptions ever found. It is thought by some to depict the unification of Upper and Lower Egypt under the king Narmer. On one side the king is depicted with the White Crown of Upper (southern) Egypt and the other side depicts the king wearing the Red Crown of Lower (northern) Egypt. The Palette was one of many discoveries located in the Temple of Horus in the city of Hierakonpolis. Today, the Narmer palette draws a significant amount of attention to historians. There are various controversies that are surrounding the legendary Narmer Palette. Among these are the following: Was this Narmer's victory over the north? Narmer Palette is often taken to be record of victory of southern kingdom over north. But the controversy on whether Nermer's victory was embedded on the palette remains unsolved.

Around 3000 B.C., Egypt emerged from the twilight of prehistory as one country, united under the single rule of a divine king. Before that, it is generally assumed that the country was divided in two parts: Upper Egypt and Lower Egypt. According to an Ancient Egyptian legend, it was an Upper Egyptian king named Menes who first united these "Two Lands". From then on, the Egyptian kings would rule Upper Egypt and Lower Egypt and one of the many names used for the country would be "Two Lands", reflecting the original duality of Egypt. The identification of Menes with one of the archaeologically attested kings of Early Dynastic Egypt has been a matter of debate among Egyptologists for quite a long time and has not yet been resolved. Some identify Menes with Narmer (3300 - 3100 B.C.), others with his probable son, Aha and others yet still see him as a mere legendary figure. The most important document pertaining to the unification of Egypt is the Narmer Palette.

The Narmer Palette, now one of the many exhibits at the Egyptian Museum in Cairo, was discovered in 1898 by the archaeologist James E. Quibell in the Upper Egyptian city of Nekhen (today's Hierakonpolis), believed to be the Pre-Dynastic capital of Upper Egypt. Quibell was excavating the royal residences of various early Egyptian kings at Hierakonpolis in Upper Egypt when he discovered that large ceremonial palette of King Narmer with other objects. The palette, which has a shield-shape, is decorated on both sides. It was once erected for display in the temple of Horus in Nekhen. It was a votive or gift offering by the King to his "father", the god Amun-Ra. Not only does it hold one of the oldest known specimens of Ancient Egyptian hieroglyphic writing, its well-preserved decoration also shows us a chapter of Ancient Egyptian history : the unification of Egypt.

There are findings that could be served the claim that it was indeed the victory over the north. But there are some possible contradictions because of the increasing evidence for gradual process of unification over some 200 years that makes an idea of single set-piece battle less likely to occur. As stated by, there are certain conflicts during the emergence of unified state, as shown by evidence from other decorated palettes, but there were probably numerous battles and skirmishes as rival chiefs struggled for territory. Some of conflict recorded on palettes may have been directed against tribes from desert regions outside Nile Valley rather than being connected with internal disputes. Further, the question on were there outsiders involved in the process was answerable with the help of other palettes discovered. The palette provides evidences that there were outsiders that are involved. The figures present in the palette are not in congruence with Egyptian people. They have curled hair and beards, and are circumcised. It is possible that some of warfare conducted against north around time of Narmer may have been directed against local population which had moved into the Delta from west. They were regarded as outsiders by the Upper Egyptian rulers. These claims are substantiated by the Narmer Palette.

The recto of the Narmer Palette is divided into two scenes. Above the top scene, the king's name is written inside a serekh (ancestor of the cartouche), flanked on each side by a cow's head, in exactly the same manner as on the back. The top scene takes up most of the recto of the Narmer Palette. Dominating the scene is a large figure of the king, with a ceremonial beard and wearing the White Crown (which is said to represent Upper Egypt), as well as the symbolic bull's tail. All the important features of the body are present: the whole eye is seen within the profile of the face; shoulders, arms and hips are frontal while the legs and feet are in profile. A solid and static, almost monumental feeling is obtained by having the weight evenly divided on both legs with one leg well in advance of the other. In his right hand the king wields a mace, ready to smash the skull of a kneeling man (possibly a Libyan) whom he holds by the hair with his left hand. The name of this kneeling man (wash) written in hieroglyphs above his head suggests that he may have been important or that it may be referring to a group of people. Above the victim's head and in front of Narmer's face, the falcon Horus of Nekhen – symbol of Egyptian royalty and protector of the king – is sitting upon the plants of a personified papyrus marshland.

The papyrus blossom in early hieroglyphs stands for the numeral one thousand – this group therefore means that the king had captured six thousand enemies. This is frequently used to symbolise Lower Egypt. Therefore the meaning of this part of the scene is quite clear : the Upper Egyptian king tramples the Lower Egyptian marshlands.

As on the back, Narmer is followed by a smaller person carrying his sandals. He is thus walking on sacred ground and is barefoot out of respect for the gods and goddesses, in order to perform the ritual act of execution. Narmer, in this way, may be dedicating his victim to the gods and goddesses perhaps thanking them for their help in conquering his foes. Below the feet of the king, below the main scene, are two naked, fallen Deltaic enemies lie helplessly on the ground, and a representation of their walled town. They too confirm the victorious imagery repeated all over the Narmer Palette.

The back of the Narmer Palette is divided into three levels. Above the top level, the king's name, "Narmer" (n'r – fish, and mr – chisel, which translates into 'Catfish'), is written inside a serekh. This serekh is flanked on each side by a cow's head, possibly a reference to either the goddess Hathor or another named Bat ["it is doubtful that there was even a goddess named Bat, although she may have been a nome deity" (Jonathan Van Lepp, personal communication)], often represented as a cow. If they do represent one, she would be the oldest known goddess of Ancient Egypt. The association of Hathor, usually represented with inwards horns, and as mother of the king is seen in most of the Egyptian art and literature. Its disposition in the upper part of the palette gives it a celestial character and proves the high esteem of the pharaoh towards her.

The Narmer Palette displays the earliest known representation of Hathor with the king. On the left hand side of the top level, the king, followed by a smaller figure carrying his sandals – known as the Sandal Bearer – is represented wearing the Red Crown of Lower Egypt. In his left hand, he holds a mace, in the other a flail, symbol of his royalty. His name is repeated just before his face. He is preceded by

56

his vizir, and by a female figure called Tjet, holding a kind of sceptre in her left hand.

All the people are represented smaller than the king. The entire procession is walking towards ten decapitated bodies – divided in two rows of five persons each, lying on the ground, with their disembodied heads between their legs. They represent the king's vanquished enemies. In the central scene, two persons tie together the elongated necks of two feline animals, which could be alluding to panthers, symbol of the eastern and western heavens. The two felines are often interpreted as the two parts of the country tied together, since they symbolise harmony and unity. It is believed that the circular depression created by the curved necks may have used to hold or make cosmetics on the palette – if ever it was really used to handle cosmetics. In the bottom scene, the Apis bull is represented trampling a scared, naked bearded Deltaic foe. The symbolism of this scene is made clear : the bull represents the king's masculinity and vigorous power, while destroying his enemies with the force of a strong bull. Some later kings would add a title such as "Victorious Bull" to their titulary.

The dominant theme however is the victory of the god incarnate over the forces of evil and chaos. The king's role was that of the preserver of unity of land and to overcome the enemies of Ma'at, goddess of Truth, Order and Justice.

The palette has raised considerable scholarly debate over the years. In general the arguments fall into one of two camps: scholars who believe that the palette is a record of actual events, and other academics who argue that it is an object designed to establish the mythology of united rule over Upper and Lower Egypt by the king. It had been thought that the palette either depicted the unification of Lower Egypt by the king of Upper Egypt, or recorded a recent military success over the Libyans, or the last stronghold of a Lower Egyptian dynasty based in Buto.

More recently scholars such as Nicholas Millet have argued that the palette does not represent a historical event (such as the unification of Egypt), but instead represents the events of the year in which the object was dedicated to the temple. Much of this doubt also comes from the fact that King Narmer did not appear in the ancient records, which signifies a great deal as Ancient Egyptians were very particular in their recording. It is certainly possible that King Narmer was an alias of Menes, hence recognized to be the first Pharaoh to have unified Egypt. To say that King Narmer has taken this role instead of King Menes would contradict with this recorded and determined history. To supply the Astronomical explanation even further is analysis that King Narmer has actual relations on the Autumn Equinox and Seth. This readily assumes Narmer as indeed, a king and a celestial counterpart as well as the anarchic God, Seth.

Another interesting interpretation may be that the Narmer Palette is an embodiment of the Sinai Peninsula, thus through this perception the palette serves to immortalize the conquest regarding this open area The Narmer Palette can be classified under two categories, historical and symbolic interpretation. The palette literally details the actual unification of Egypt shown from several iconographies. Thus, Narmer may be a king of Egypt, or a much minor ruler. But whatever those interpretations are, the facts still remain as an irony that the Narmer palette could solely serve the answer.

Starchild Skull

The Starchild skull is an abnormal human-like skull which was found in Mexico. Its origin and nature are contested by scientists and paranormal enthusiasts. The starchild skull came into the possession of Lloyd Pye, a writer and lecturer in the field of alternative knowledge, in February 1999.

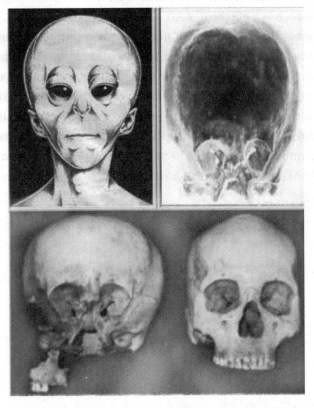

According to Pye, the skull was found around 1930 in a mine tunnel about 100 miles (200 km) southwest of the Mexican city of Chihuahua, Chihuahua, buried alongside a normal human skeleton which was exposed and lying supine on the surface of the tunnel. The skull is abnormal in several aspects. A dentist determined that it was a child's skull, due to unerupted teeth being impacted in the associated upper right maxilla found with the skull. However, the volume of the interior of the starchild skull is 1600 cubic centimetres, which is 200 cm3 larger than the average adult's brain, and 400 cm3 larger than an adult of the same approximate size.

The orbits are oval and shallow, with the optic nerve canal situated at the bottom of the orbit instead of at the back. There are no frontal sinuses. The back of the skull is flattened, but not by artificial means. The skull consists of calcium hydroxyapatite, the normal material of mammalian bone, but there is an overload of collagen in it, much more than is usual for human bone. Carbon 14 dating was performed twice, the first on the normal human skull at the University of California at Riverside in 1999, and on the Starchild skull in 2004 at Beta Analytic in Miami, the largest radiocarbon dating laboratory in the world. Both independent tests gave a result of 900 years ± 40 years since death. DNA testing at Trace Genetics in 2003 recovered mitochondrial DNA and determined that the child had a human mother, though it was not the child of the skull found with it.

Nampa Image

A small human image, skillfully formed in clay, was found in 1889 at Nampa, Idaho. The figurine was found at over 300-foot level of a well boring which would appear to place its age far before the expected arrival of man in this part of the world. Other than Homo sapiens sapiens, no hominid is known to have fashioned works of art like the Nampa figurine. The evidence therefore suggests that humans of the modern type were living in America around 2 million years ago, at the Plio-Pleistocene boundary.

In 1887 James A. Pinney, Nathan Falk, Joseph Perrault, John Bernard, and M. A. Kurtz formed a company to locate artesian water at the new frontier town of Nampa, Idaho. By July of 1889, one of the owners of the drilling company, Mark A. Kurtz, was checking the material brought up by a sand pump from a layer of clay over 300 feet down in the well boring. A strange object came into his hands. On washing it, he found it was a small human figurine.

Kurtz later showed the figurine to Charles F. Adams, president of the Union Pacific Railroad, who happened to be passing through Idaho.

Adams, who had recently read a book by G. F. Wright, wrote to Wright about the discovery. Wright, from the East Coast of the United States, wrote to Kurtz, requesting a photograph of the artefact. Kurtz replied that there was no way for him to make a photograph, so he sent Wright the figurine. Wright noted: "The object is about an inch and a half long, and remarkable for the perfection with which it represents the human form." He added, "It was a female figure, and had the lifelike lineaments in the parts which were finished that would do credit to the classic centres of art." Wright also examined the borehole to see if the figurine could have slipped down from a higher level. He stated: "To answer objections it will be well to give the facts more fully. The well was six inches in diametre and was tubed with heavy iron tubing, which was driven down, from the top, and screwed together, section by section, as progress was made. Thus it was impossible for anything to work in from the sides. The drill was not used after penetrating the lava deposit near the surface, but the tube was driven down, and the included material brought out from time to time by use of a sand pump."

The object was not of recent manufacture. It was deeply coloured with the iron oxides characteristic of the deposits from the 300-foot level. Wright showed the object to archaeologist F. W. Putnam of Harvard University. "Upon showing the object to Professor F. W. Putnam," wrote Wright, "he at once directed attention to the character of the incrustations of iron upon the surface as indicative of a relic of considerable antiquity. There were patches of anhydrous red oxide of iron in protected places upon it, such as could not have been formed upon any fraudulent object. In visiting the locality in 1890, while on the ground, to compare the discolouration of the oxide upon the image with that upon the clay balls still found among the debris which has come from the well, and ascertained it to be as nearly identical as it is possible to be. These confirmatory evidences, in connection with the very satisfactory character of the evidence furnished by the parties who made the discovery, and confirmed by Mr. G. M. Cumming, of Boston (at that time superintendent of that division of the Oregon Short Line Railroad, and who knew all the parties, and was upon the ground a day or two after the discovery) placed the genuineness of the discovery beyond reasonable doubt. To this evidence is to be added, also, the general conformity of the object to other relics of man which have been found beneath the lava deposits on the Pacific coast. The Nampa image is also similar to the famous Willendorf Venus, thought to be about 30,000 years old."

According to current Darwinian theories of evolution, figurines like the Idaho image are made only by humans of the modern type, who came into existence only about 200,000 years ago. The oldest statues of human figures of a degree of artistry similar to that of the Nampa image only go back to the Late Paleolithic period of Europe, about 20,000 or 30,000 years. In ancient Sanskrit writings of India, however, humans have been present since the beginning of life on earth. There are figures of gods and goddesses in Indian temples that, according to traditional sources, are as old as the Nampa image and older.

The Nampa figurine strongly challenges the evolutionary scenario was noted by W. H. Holmes of the Smithsonian Institution. In 1919, Holmes wrote in his Handbook of Aboriginal American Antiquities: "According to Emmons, the formation in which the pump was operating is of late Tertiary or early Quaternary age; and the apparent improbability of the occurrence of a well-modeled human figure in deposits of such great antiquity has led to grave doubt about its authenticity." Holmes think that it must be slipped down from a higher level. Evidence that contradicts evolutionary preconceptions about the antiquity of the human species is often rejected, just for that reason alone.

If Holmes could have demonstrated that he could in that area find some place where he could drop a figurine and have it go down 300 feet into the ground by some natural pathway through a 15-foot layer of basalt, and further down to the 300-foot level, that might constitute some real evidence in support of his theory. But no such evidence was provided. We also have to take into account the testimony of Dr. Putnam and Dr. Jewett that the object was of considerable antiquity. Today the Nampa image is kept in storage at the Idaho State Historical Society in Boise, Idaho.

Map of the Creator

In 2002 the scientists of Bashkir State University in Russia claim that they found an undeniable proof of the existence of a highly advanced civilization in the distant past. Their evidence is a stone slab with weight more than a ton, (with dimension approximately five feet long by three-and-a-half feet wide, and six inches thick) its age estimated, probably millions of years. The stone slab was found beneath the house of one of the community leader in the city of Ufa, the surface of the slab showed an amazing accuracy of 3D relief map of the Ural Mountain. The discoverer eventually called it "Map of the Creator."

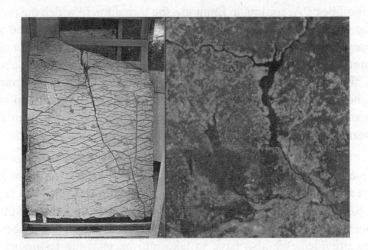

Alexander Chuvyrov, professor of physics and mathematics, the discoverer, said that during his research of the traces of ancient Chinese influence in the region and had heard the stories of the 20th century researchers from various ancient slabs. Even though he's very interested, he barely couldn't find any single stone slab, until one day when a head of the local agricultural committee told him that there is one stone slab beneath his house.

After recover it, Chuvyrov being shocked because he found a map that most accurately described many existing natural features, and many no longer exist, including the discovery of a system of canals, dams and reservoirs, and the inscriptions in an unknown language.

It was first discovered in July 1999, and has been subjected to numerous test by the scientist of Russia. The results are surprising, to say the least. The age determinations have been based on radio-carbon dating test, however the origin of the stone is still questionable. The technical difficulties in creating such an accurate map of this discovery is much more than any ancient culture that previously believes by orthodox scientists which have occupied the region, or elsewhere, anywhere on Earth.

This map is still very difficult to reproduce. Some researchers believe that this slab is a fragment of a complete map of the earth.

Malta's Long-Headed Skull

Long ago in the megalithic temple of Hal Saflieni, in Malta, were buried men with extraordinary cranial volume. Their skulls seem to observers today belong to a truly alien stock. A similarity with skulls from Egypt and South America found with this particular deformity – ancient (from approximately 3000 B.C.), yet unique in medical pathology – suggests this could be an extraordinary discovery. Was this skull the result of an ancient genetic mutation between different races or something else? Before 1985 a number of these skulls, found in prehistoric Maltese temples at Taxien, Ggantja and Hal Saflieni, were displayed in the Archaeological Museum of the Valletta. A few years ago, though, they were removed and placed in storage. The public has not seen them since. Only the photographs taken by Maltese researcher Dr. Anton Mifsud and his colleague Dr. Charles Savona Ventura remain to testify of their existence and as proof of their extraordinary characteristics.

All skulls were found in the Hal Saflieni hypogeum, where a sacred well was dedicated to the Mother Goddess and where the small statue of a sleeping goddess associated with a snake inscribed relic was also found. The skulls were brought out one at a time The cranium showed a very pronounced dolichocephalous, in other words, a lengthened posterior part of the skullcap, besides the lack of median knitting, technically named "sagitta." This last detail has been called "impossible" by the medics and anatomists. It does not have (as far as known) any analogous cases in international pathological medical literature. The anomalous nature of the finding is underscored by a natural lengthening of the cranium in the occipital area (not due to bandaging or boards like those used in pre- Columbian civilizations).

Malta and Gozo have been very important centres since prehistoric times, places where "medical cures" were sought from oracles and in ritual encounters with the priests of the goddess. There existed, on both islands, many sanctuaries and thaumaturgic centres, where priests surrounded the healing goddess, in direct support of her divinity. It is well known that, in antiquity, the serpent was associated with the goddess and her healing capacities. The snake also belongs to the subterranean world. Therefore, a hypogeum dedicated to the goddess and the water cult was the right place for a sacerdotal group defined, in all the most ancient cultures, as the "serpent priests" (an epithet still in use for shamans). The long head and drawn features must have given an almost serpent-like appearance, stretching the eyes and skin. Lacking the lower part, but the hypothesis seems plausible. Such deformities would certainly have created walking problems, forcing him almost to slither! The lack of the cranium's median knitting and therefore, the impossibility of the brain's consistent, radial expansion in the skullcap must have caused terrible agony from infancy, but could have enhanced the visions considered proof of a bond with the goddess.

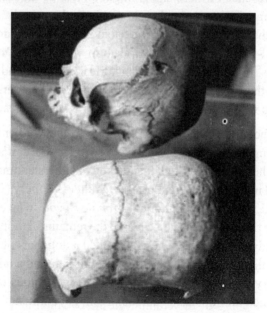

It's worth emphasizing that one of these skulls showed unmistakable signs of surgical intervention. The outlines of three small holes, made in the occipital bone called inion, had time to cicatrize, therefore the patient survived the operation although such intervention surely would have undermined his motor faculties. But there is more.

A fair part of the 7000 skeletons dug out of the Hal Saflieni hypogeum and examined by Themistocles Zammit in 1921 presented artificially performed deformations. A skeleton of the group that was unearthed by the archaeologist, Brochtorff Circle, shows clear signs of intentional deformation through bondage. These deformations could have occurred for various reasons: initiation, matrimony, solar ritual, punishment for social transgressions, etc. All the tribal apparatus of incisions, perforations, partial or total removals, cauterizations, abrasions, insertions of extraneous bodies in muscles, like the modification of bodies for magical, medical or cosmetic purposes, were part of cruel practices, but possibly "with best intentions" for the community.

In Malta, all this was practiced by a mysterious populace that erected gigantic temples to the Mother Goddess between 4100 and 2500 B.C. The presence of these skulls might be that of the last exponents of the most ancient sacerdotal caste that built the megalithic temples. The skulls that have been found are dated 2500 B.C. (but may be even older. No C-14 test was done) – a date in which Malta's megalithic history ends, initiating a period of historical darkness and absence of population that was to last about 300 years, until the arrival of the Phoenicians who began to make Malta their Mediterranean outpost.

The Phoenicians also erected temples to the Mother Goddess in Malta, calling her Astarte, the snakefaced Goddess. But it's the date of 2500 B.C. that presents a fundamental key to understanding who these longheaded individuals were. Professor Walter B. Emery (1903-1971), the famous Egyptologist, author of "*Archaic Egypt*," who excavated at Saqqara in the '30s, indeed discovered the remains of individuals who lived in predynastic epoch. These presented a dolichocephalous skull, larger than that of the local ethnic group, fair hair and a taller, heavier build. Emery declared that this stock wasn't indigenous to Egypt but had performed an important sacerdotal and governmental role in this country. This race kept its distance from the common people, blending only with the aristocratic classes, and the scholar associated them with the Shemsu Hor, the "disciples of Horus." The Shemsu Hor are recognized as the dominant sacerdotal caste in predynastic Egypt (until approximately 3000 B.C.), being mentioned in the Turin papyrus and the list of the kings of Abydos.

It's interesting to note that Emery writes: "Towards the end of the IV millennium B.C. the people known as the Disciples of Horus appear as a highly dominant aristocracy that governed all of Egypt. The theory of the existence of this race is supported by the discovery in the predynastic tombs, in the northern part of Upper Egypt, of the anatomical remains of individuals with bigger skulls and builds than the native population, with so much difference as to exclude any hypothetical common racial strain. The fusion of the two races must have come about in ages that concurred, more or less, with the unification of the two Egyptian Kingdoms." Therefore, what occurred in Malta is also reflected in Egypt.

It can be concluded that these serpent-priests were the most ancient race that first occupied the fertile half-moon area (particularly Anatolia and Kurdistan) and Egypt (following migrations dating back 6000-4000 B.C.) until reaching Malta to disappear around 2500 B.C. but this culture survived in the Middle East and probably included one of the most famous and yet mysterious pharaohs of Egypt – Akhenaton. Portrayed in statues and bas-reliefs with his family was an individual of lengthened head and human face – like that found in the pre-dynastic Egyptian stock mentioned by Emery – but closely resembling the long-skulled individuals of Malta. X-rays of Tuthankamun's skull, Akhenaton's son, indeed, showed a dolichocephalous cranium. Substantially, the Maltese craniums appear to be relics – though, archaeologically still not understood – of a sacerdotal race that, in Egypt and Malta, from archaic ages, survived till 2500 B.C.

Kusanagi-no-Tsurugi

Kusanagi-no-Tsurugi is a legendary Japanese sword as important to Japan's history as Excalibur is to Britain's, and is one of three Imperial Regalia of Japan. It was originally called Ama-no-Murakumo-no-Tsurugi ("Sword of the Gathering Clouds of Heaven") but its name was late changed to the more popular Kusanagi-no-Tsurugi. It is also called Tsumugari-no-Tachi. The history of the Kusanagi-no-Tsurugi extends into legend. According to Kojiki, the Japanese god Susa-no-o encountered a grieving family of kunitsukami ("gods of the land") headed by Ashinazuchi in Izumo province. When Susa-no-o inquired of Ashinazuchi, he told him that his family was being ravaged by the fearsome Yamata-no-Orochi, an eight-headed serpent of Koshi, who consumed seven of the family's eight daughters and that the creature was coming for his final daughter, Kushinada-hime.

Susa-no-o investigated the creature, and after an abortive encounter he returned with a plan to defeat it. In return, he asked for Kushinada-hime's hand in marriage, which was agreed. Transforming her temporarily into a comb (one interpreter reads this section as "using a comb he turns into [masquerades as] Kushinada-hime") to have her company during battle, he detailed his plan into steps. He instructed the preparation of eight vats of sake (rice wine) to be put on individual platforms positioned behind a fence with eight gates. The monster took the bait and put each of its heads through each gate. With this distraction, Susa-no-o attacked and slew the beast. He chopped off each head and then proceeded to the tails. In the fourth tail, he discovered a great sword inside the body of the serpent which he called Ama-no-Murakumo-no-Tsurugi, which he presented to the goddess, Amaterasu to settle an old grievance.

Generations later, in the reign of the Twelfth Emperor, Keikō, the sword was given to the great warrior, Yamato Takeru as part of a pair of gifts given by his aunt, Yamatohime the Shrine Maiden of Ise Shrine, to protect her nephew in times of peril. These gifts came in handy when Yamato Takeru was lured onto an open grassland during a hunting expedition by a treacherous warlord. The lord had fiery arrows to ignite the grass and trap Yamato Takeru in the field so that he would burn to death. He also killed the warrior's horse to prevent his escape.

Desperately, Yamato Takeru used the Ama-no-Murakumo-no-Tsurugi to cut back the grass and remove fuel from the fire, but in doing so, he discovered that the sword enabled him to control the wind and cause it to move in the direction of his swing. Taking advantage of this magic, Yamato Takeru used his other gift, fire strikers, to enlarge the fire in the direction of the lord and his men, and he used the winds controlled by the sword to sweep the blaze toward them. In triumph, Yamato Takeru renamed the sword Kusanagi-no-Tsurugi (lit. "Grasscutter Sword") to commemorate his narrow escape and victory. Eventually, Yamato Takeru married and later fell in battle with a monster, after ignoring his wife's advice to take the Kusanagi-no-Tsurugi with him.

Although the sword is mentioned in the Kojiki, this book is a collection of Japanese myths and is not considered a historical document. The first reliable historical mention of the sword is in the Nihonshoki. Although the Nihonshiki also contains mythological stories that are not considered reliable history, it records some events that were contemporary or nearly contemporary to its writing, and these sections of the book are considered historical. In the Nihonshoki, the Kusanagi was removed from the Imperial palace in 688, and moved to Atsuta Shrine after the sword was blamed for causing Emperor Temmu to fall ill. Along with the jewel and the mirror, it is one of the three imperial regalia of Japan, the sword representing the virtue of valor. Kusanagi is allegedly kept at Atsuta Shrine to this day, although it is not available for public display, and its existence cannot be confirmed. It is recorded that during the Edo period, a Shinto priest[who?] claimed to have seen the sword. According to him, the sword was about 84 cm long, shaped like calamus, fashioned in a white metallic colour, and well maintained. Another record claims that this priest died from the curse and the power of the sword, but this is most likely a story that was spread to emphasize its power. In recent times, Japan's nationally run broadcasting station, NHK, went to Atsuta Shrine to videotape the sword but were turned away.

Although some sword may be held by the Atsuta shrine, it is somewhat unlikely to be the legendary Kusanagi. In *The Tale of the Heike*, a collection of oral stories transcribed in 1371, the sword is lost at sea after the defeat of the Heike clan in the Battle of Dan-no-ura, a naval battle that ended in the defeat of the Heike clan forces and the child Emperor Antoku at the hands of Minamoto no Yoshitsune. In the tale, upon hearing of the Navy's defeat, the Emperor's grandmother led the Emperor and his entourage to commit suicide by drowning in the waters of the strait along with the three imperial regalia, including Kusanagi. Although the Minamoto troops managed to stop a handful of them and recovered two of the three regalia, Kusanagi was said to have been lost forever. Although written about historical events, The Tale of the Heike is a collection of epic poetry passed down orally and written down nearly 200 years after the actual events, so its reliability as a historical document is questionable.

According to some records, the Tenth Emperor, Emperor Sujin, is reported to have ordered the fashioning of a replica of Kusanagi. However, this information was reportedly only made public after it was known that the sword had been stolen. The imperial household claimed that it was the replica which was stolen, but it is just as likely that the replica was made after the fact to replace the irrecoverable sword. It should be noted that Emperor Sujin is considered a "legendary Emperor" by historians, because of a lack of sufficient evidence to assign him to a historical period. Another story holds that the sword was reportedly stolen again in the sixth century by a Chinese monk.

However, his ship allegedly sank at sea, allowing the sword to wash ashore at Ise, where it was recovered by Shinto priests. Given the somewhat fantastic nature of this story, its historical accuracy is questionable. Due to the refusal of Shinto priests to show the sword, and the rather sketchy nature of its historical references, the current state of or even the existence at all of the sword as a historical artefact cannot be confirmed. The last appearance of the sword was in 1989 when Emperor Akihito ascended to the throne, the sword (including the jewel and the Emperor's two seals) were shrouded in packages.

The Lost Gospel

In December 1945 an Arab peasant made an astonishing archaeological discovery. A collection of early Christian Gnostic texts discovered near the Upper Egyptian town of Nag Hammadi. That year, thirteen leather-bound papyrus codices buried in a sealed jar were found. The Nag Hammadi Gospel (popularly known as The Gnostic Gospels)

 comprised fifty-two mostly Gnostic tractates (treatises), but they also include three works belonging to the Corpus Hermeticum and a partial translation/alteration of Plato's Republic. Rumours obscured the circumstances of this find,

perhaps because the discovery was accidental and its sale on the black market illegal. In his "Introduction" to The Nag Hammadi Library in English, James Robinson suggests that these codices may have belonged to a nearby Pachomian monastery, and were buried after Bishop Athanasius condemned the uncritical use of non-canonical books in his Festal Letter of 367 AD. The contents of the codices were written in Coptic, though the works were probably all translations from Greek. The best-known of these works is probably the Gospel of Thomas, of which the Nag Hammadi codices contain the only complete text.

After the discovery it was recognized that fragments of these sayings attributed to Jesus appeared in manuscripts discovered at Oxyrhynchus in 1898, and matching quotations were recognized in other early Christian sources. Subsequently, a 1st or 2nd century date of composition circa 80 AD for the lost Greek originals of the Gospel of Thomas has been proposed, though this is disputed by many if not the majority of biblical matter researchers. The once buried manuscripts themselves date from the 3rd and 4th centuries.

For years even the identity of the discoverer remained unknown. One rumour held that he was a blood avenger; another, that he had made the find near the town of Naj Hammadi at the Jabal al-Tarif, a mountain honeycombed with more than 150 caves. Originally natural, some of these caves were cut and painted and used as grave sites as early as the sixth dynasty, some 4,300 years ago. Thirty years later the discoverer himself, Muhammad Ali al-Samman, told what happened. Shortly before he and his brothers avenged their father's murder in a blood feud, they had saddled their camels and gone out to the Jabal to dig for sabakh, a soft soil they used to fertilize their crops. Digging around a massive boulder, they hit a red earthenware jar, almost a metre high. Muhammad Ali hesitated to break the jar. But realizing that it might also contain gold, he raised his mattock, smashed the jar, and discovered inside thirteen papyrus books, bound in leather. Muhammad Ali asked the priest, al-Qummus Basiliyus Abd al-Masïh, to keep one or more for him.

During the time that Muhammad Ali and his brothers were being interrogated for murder, Raghib, a local history teacher, had seen one of the books, and suspected that it had value. Having received one from al- Qummus Basiliyus, Raghib sent it to a friend in Cairo to find out its worth. Sold on the black market through antiquities dealers in Cairo, the manuscripts soon attracted the attention of officials of the Egyptian government. Through circumstances of high drama, as we shall see, they bought one and confiscated ten and a half of the thirteen leather-bound books, called codices, and deposited them in the Coptic Museum in Cairo. But a large part of the thirteenth codex, containing five extraordinary texts, was smuggled out of Egypt and offered for sale in America.

Word of this codex soon reached Professor Gilles Quispel, distinguished historian of religion at Utrecht, in the Netherlands. Excited by the discovery, Quispel urged the Jung Foundation in Zürich to buy the codex. But discovering, when he succeeded, that some pages were missing, he flew to Egypt in the spring of 1955 to try to find them in the Coptic Museum. Arriving in Cairo, he went at once to the museum, borrowed photographs of some of the texts, and hurried back to his hotel to decipher them. Tracing out the first line, Quispel was startled, then incredulous, to read: "These are the secret words which the living Jesus spoke, and which the twin, Judas Thomas, wrote down." Quispel

knew that his colleague H.C. Puech, using notes from another French scholar, Jean Doresse, had identified the opening lines with fragments of a Greek Gospel of Thomas discovered in the 1890s. But the discovery of the whole text raised new questions: Did Jesus have a twin brother, as this text implies? Could the text be an authentic record of Jesus's sayings? According to its title, it contained the Gospel According to Thomas; yet, unlike the Gospels of the New Testament, this text identified itself as a secret gospel.

Quispel also discovered that it contained many sayings known from the New Testament; but these sayings, placed in unfamiliar contexts, suggested other dimensions of meaning. Other passages, Quispel found, differed entirely from any known Christian tradition: The "living Jesus," for example, speaks in sayings as cryptic and compelling as Zen koans: "Jesus said, 'If you bring forth what is within you, what you bring forth will save you. If you do not bring forth what is within you, what you do not bring forth will destroy you.'" What Quispel held in his hand, the Gospel of Thomas, was only one of the fifty-two texts discovered at Nag Hammadi. Bound into the same volume with it is the Gospel of Philip, which attributes to Jesus acts and sayings quite different from those in the New Testament:

"... the companion of the [Savior is] Mary Magdalene. [But Christ loved] her more than [all] the disciples, and used to kiss her [often] on her [mouth]. The rest of [the disciples were offended.] ... They said to him, 'Why do you love her more than all of us?' The Savior answered and said to them, Why do I not love you as [I love] her?" Other sayings in this collection criticize common Christian beliefs, such as the virgin birth or the bodily resurrection, as naïve misunderstandings. Bound together with these gospels is the Apocryphon (literally, "secret book") of John, which opens with an offer to reveal "the mysteries [and the] things hidden in silence" which Jesus taught to his disciple John.

76

Muhammad 'Ali later admitted that some of the texts were lost – burned up or thrown away. But what remains is astonishing: some fifty-two texts from the early centuries of the Christian era, including a collection of early Christian gospels, previously unknown. ... What Muhammad 'Ali discovered at Nag Hammadi, it soon became clear, were Coptic translations, made about 1,500 years ago, of still more ancient manuscripts. The originals themselves had been written in Greek, the language of the New Testament: As Doresse, Puech, and Quispel had recognized, part of one of them had been discovered by archaeologists about fifty years earlier, when they found a few fragments of the original Greek version of the Gospel of Thomas. About the dating of the manuscripts themselves there is little debate.

Examination of the datable papyrus used to thicken the leather bindings, and of the Coptic script, place them about A.D. 350-400. But scholars sharply disagree about the dating of the original texts. Some of them can hardly be later than about A.D. 120-150, since Irenaeus, the orthodox Bishop of Lyon, writing about 180, declares that heretics "boast that they possess more gospels than there really are " and complains that in his time such writings already have won wide circulation, from Gaul through Rome, Greece, and Asia Minor. Quispel and his collaborators, who first published the Gospel of Thomas, suggested the date of about 140 for the original. ... But recently Professor Helmut Koester of Harvard University has suggested that the collection of sayings in the Gospel of Thomas, although compiled about 140, may include some traditions even older than the Gospels of the New Testament, "possibly as early as the second half of the first century" (50-100) – as early as, or earlier, than Mark, Matthew, Luke, and John. ...

Why were these texts buried – and why have they remained virtually unknown for nearly 2,000 years? Their suppression as banned documents, and their burial on the cliff at Nag Hammadi, it turns out, were both part of a struggle critical for the formation of early Christianity. Some scholars said the Nag Hammadi texts, and others like them, which circulated at the beginning of the Christian era, were denounced as heresy by orthodox Christians in the middle of the second century.

Aluminium Wedge of Aiud

The Aluminum Wedge of Aiud, also known as the Object of Aiud, is a wedge-shaped object found 2 kilometres East of Aiud, Romania, on the banks of the Mures river in 1974. According to an article written by Boczor Iosif, a contributor to Hungarian paranormal magazines, it was found under 35 feet of sand and along side 2 mastodon bones. His article also claims it was found in 1973. For three reasons some  claim the wedge is proof that aliens came to visit Earth in the past. An unnamed aeronautical engineer said it resembled the foot of landing gear not unlike the current space vehicles at the time, only smaller. This was corroborated by Florin Gheorghita, a known ufologist in Romania. The fact that it was found in the same layer as mastodon bones, and assuming it was found in original context, would make it at least 11,000 years old. The third reason people believed that this was from an alien ship was because aluminum was not even discovered until 1808 and could not be produced in mass until 1885. Therefore, because it looks like landing gear, it was found with mastodon bones and the oxide dated to at least 300 years old (before aluminum on earth), it was from an alien spaceship. Most scientists believe the wedge was made here on earth and its purpose is just not yet identified. Not much information is to be found on this subject. The lack of data can possibly be explained by the imposed restrictions on archaeology and history by the communist rule of the time. Aluminum requires 1,000 degrees of heat to be produced. The aluminum wedge of Aiud remains a mystery.

Klerksdorp Sphere

Klerksdorp spheres are small objects, often spherical to disc-shaped, that have been collected by miners and rockhounds from 3-billion-year-old pyrophyllite deposits mined by Wonderstone Ltd., near Ottosdal, South Africa. They have been cited by alternative researchers and reporters in books, popular articles, and many web pages, as inexplicable out of place artefacts that could only have been manufactured by intelligent beings. Geologists who have studied these objects argue that the objects are not manufactured, but are rather the result of natural processes. Roelf Marx, curator of the museum of Klerksdorp, South Africa, where some of the spheres are housed, said: "The spheres are a complete mystery. They look man-made, yet at the time in Earth's history when they came to rest in this rock no intelligent life existed. They're nothing like I have ever seen before."

According to an article by J. Jimison, the spheres are of two types – "one of solid bluish metal with white flecks, and another which is a hollow ball filled with a white spongy centre." On a letter dated September 12, 1984 Roelf Marx said : "There is nothing scientific published about the globes, but the facts are: They are found in pyrophyllite, which is mined near the little town of Ottosdal in the Western Transvaal. This pyrophyllite is a quite soft secondary mineral with a count of only 3 on the Mohs scale and was formed by sedimentation about 2.8 billion years ago. On the other hand the globes, which have a fibrous structure on the inside with a shell around it, are very hard and cannot be scratched, even by steel." The Mohs scale of hardness is named after Friedrich Mohs, who chose ten minerals as references points for comparative hardness, with talc the softest (1) and diamond the hardest (10).

A. Bisschoff, a professor of geology at the University of Potchefstroom, said that the spheres were "limonite concretions." Limonite is a kind of iron ore. A concretion is a compact, rounded rock mass formed by localized cementation around a nucleus. One problem with the hypothesis that the objects are limonite concretions concerns their hardness. As noted above, the metallic spheres cannot be scratched with a steel point, indicating they are extremely hard. But standard references on minerals state that limonite registers only 4 to 5.5 on the Mohs scale, indicating a relatively low degree of hardness.

Furthermore, limonite concretions usually occur in groups, like masses of soap bubbles stuck together. They do not, it seems, normally appear isolated and perfectly round, as is the case with the objects in question. Neither do they normally appear with parallel grooves encircling them.

All of the specimens of these objects, which were cut open by Heinrich, exhibited an extremely well-defined radial structure terminating on either the centre or centres of a Klerksdorp sphere. Through petrographic and X-Ray diffraction analyses of specimens of these objects Heinrich found that they consist either of hematite (Fe_2O_3) or wollastonite ($CaSiO_3$) mixed with minor amounts of hematite and goethite ($FeOOH$). Observations by Cairncross and Nel and others indicated that many of the Klerksdorp spheres found in unaltered pyrophyllite consist of pyrite (FeS_2). The colour of the specimens studied by Heinrich ranged from dark reddish brown, red, to dusky red. The colour of those objects composed of pyrite is not known.

For the purposes of this study, it is the sphere with three parallel grooves around its equator that most concerns us. Even if it is conceded that the sphere itself is a limonite concretion, one still must account for the three parallel grooves. In the absence of a satisfactory natural explanation, the evidence is somewhat mysterious, leaving open the possibility that the South African grooved sphere – found in a mineral deposit 2.8 billion years old – was made by an intelligent being.

Ancient Jade Disc

Mysterious ancient discs made from nephrite jade discovered in China (2005) are raising scientific eyebrows in China and elsewhere. Among the earliest surviving Chinese artefacts, the discs are called 'Bi' and have been associated by some scholars with the Shang Dynasty (16th-11th century B.C.); however, they may be much older, representing neolithic art from 6000 to 2000 B.C. Showing clear evidence of advanced precision tooling, though, the 'Bi' discs present scientists with an unexplainable anomaly.

It is difficult, if not impossible, to imagine how they could have been made with the primitive stone tools and abrasives usually associated with the period. The original function and significance of the bi are unknown, as the Neolithic cultures have left no written history. From these earliest times they were buried with the dead, as a sky symbol, accompanying the dead into the after world or "sky", with the cong which connected the body with the earth. They were placed ceremonially on the body in the grave of persons of high social status.

Bi are sometimes found near the stomach and chest in neolithic burials. Jade, like bi disks, has been used throughout Chinese history to indicate an individual of moral quality, and has also served as an important symbol of rank. They were used in worship and ceremony – as ceremonial items they symbolised the ranks of emperor, king, duke, marquis, viscount, and baron with four different kweis and two different bi disks.

Bi that found recently in China are flat with a round central hole. In some respects they resemble a phonograph disc or a CD Rom. And, in fact, some believe that data of some type may actually be encoded in the concentric circular grooves. New laser technology has shown some promise in extracting intelligent information from the indentations. Some experts have speculated that the discs may be of an extraterrestrial origin and have pointed to a similarity with the so-called Dropa Stones of China which are claimed to be 10,000 to 12,000 years old.

The Iron Pillar of Delhi

In the southern district of New Delhi is the famed Iron Pillar, generally believed to date from the fourth century A.D., but said by some scholars to be over four thousand years old. It was built as a memorial to a king named Chandra. It is a solid shaft of iron, sixteen inches in diametre and twenty three feet high. It has attracted the attention of both archaeologists and metallurgists, as it has withstood corrosion for over 1600 years in the open air. The pillar defies explanation, not only for not having rusted, but because it is apparently made of 98% pure wrought iron, and is a testament to the high level of skill achieved by ancient Indian ironsmiths, which can only be produced today in tiny quantities by electrolysis. The technique used to cast such a gigantic, solid iron pillar is also a mystery, as it would be difficult to construct another of this size even today.

The pillar – seven metres (23 feet) high and weighing more than six tons – is said to have been fashioned at the time of Chandragupta II Vikramaditya (375–413), though other authorities give dates as early as 912 BCE, initially stood in the centre of a Jain temple complex housing twenty-seven temples that were destroyed by Qutb-ud-din Aybak, and their material was used in building the Qutub Minar and Quwwat-ul-Islam mosque. Made up of 98% pure wrought iron, it is 7.21m (23 feet 8 inches) high, with 93 cm (36.6 inches) buried below the present floor level, and has a diametre of 41 cm (16 inches) at the bottom which tapers towards the upper end. The pillar was manufactured by forge welding. The temperatures required to form such a pillar by forge welding could only have been achieved by the combustion of coal.

The mystery of the use of iron in Asia especially in India is one that largely baffles modern metallurgists. It is assumed that these countries developed iron and other metallurgical skills after the west, but the evidence points otherwise. Nikolass van der Merwe gives the orthodox view: "Spreading east from the Mediterranean, iron was diffused throughout most of Asia before the Christian era. By 1100 B.C. it was in use in Persia, from where it spread to Pakistan and India. The date of the arrival of iron in India is still a matter of some dispute; until recently, iron was assumed to have reached Northern India around 500 B.C., where it appears at the sites of Taxila, Histinapura, and Ahichatra in association with the distinctive 'Northern Black Polished' pottery type.

To add to the evidence that ancient India had highly advanced smelting works, the monthly Motilal Banarsidass Newsletter from New Delhi, India reported in its July 1998 edition that findings by the State Archaeology Department after excavations in Sonebhadra district, Lucknow, India, may revolutionize history as regards to the antiquity of iron. The department has unearthed iron artefacts dated between 1200 – 1300 B.C. at the Raja Nal Ka Tila site in the Karmanasa river valley of north Sonebhadra. Said the newsletter, "Radio carbon dating of one of the samples done by the Birbal Sahani Institute of Palaeobotany has established that it belongs to 1300 B.C., taking the antiquity of iron at least 400 years back, even by conservative estimates. This date of iron is one of the earliest in the Indian subcontinent." And, these are conservative estimates indeed. There is considerable evidence that mining and iron working have gone on long before 1300 B.C.

The pillar bears a Sanskrit inscription in Brahmi script which states that it was erected as a standard in honour of Lord Vishnu. It also praises the valor and qualities of a king referred to simply as Chandra, who has been identified with the Gupta King Chandragupta II Vikramaditya (375-413). The inscription reads (in the translation given in the tablets erected by Pandit Banke Rai in 1903):

"He, on whose arm fame was inscribed by the sword, when, in battle in the Vanga countries (Bengal), he kneaded (and turned) back with (his) breast the enemies who, uniting together, came against (him);-he, by whom, having crossed in warfare the seven mouths of the (river) Sindhu, the Vahlikas were conquered;-he, by the breezes of whose prowess the southern ocean is even still perfumed;- (Line 3.)-He, the remnant of the great zeal of whose energy, which utterly destroyed (his) enemies, like (the remnant of the great glowing heat) of a burned-out fire in a great forest, even now leaves not the earth; though he, the king, as if wearied, has quit this earth, and has gone to the other world, moving in (bodily) from to the land (of paradise) won by (the merit of his) actions, (but) remaining on (this) earth by (the memory of his) fame;- (L. 5.)-By him, the king,-who attained sole supreme sovereignty in the world, acquired by his own arm and (enjoyed) for a very long time; (and) who, having the name of Chandra, carried a beauty of countenance like (the beauty of) the full-moon,-having in faith fixed his mind upon (the god) Vishnu, this lofty standard of the divine Vishnu was set up on the hill (called) Vishnupada."

In a report published in the journal Current Science, R. Balasubramaniam of the IIT Kanpur try to explains how the pillar's resistance to corrosion is due to a passive protective film at the iron-rust interface. The presence of second phase particles (slag and unreduced iron oxides) in the microstructure of the iron, that of high amounts of phosphorus in the metal, and the alternate wetting and drying existing under atmospheric conditions, are the three main factors in the three-stages formation of that protective passive film.

Lepidocrocite and goethite are the first amorphous iron oxyhydroxides that appear upon oxidation of iron. High corrosion rates are initially observed. Then an essential chemical reaction intervenes:

86

slag and unreduced iron oxides (second phase particles) in the iron microstructure alter the polarization characteristics and enrich the metal–scale interface with P, thus indirectly promoting passivation of the iron (cessation of rusting activity). The second phase particles act as a cathode, and the metal itself serves as anode, for a mini-galvanic corrosion reaction during environment exposure. Part of the initial iron oxyhydroxides is also transformed into magnetite, which somewhat slows down the process of corrosion.

But the ongoing reduction of lepidocrocite, and the diffusion of oxygen and complementary corrosion through the cracks and pores in the rust, should still contribute to the corrosion mechanism from atmospheric conditions. In fact the pillar has never rusted for centuries.

The pillar stands as mute testimony to the highly advanced scientific knowledge that was known in antiquity, and not duplicated until recent times. Yet still, there is no satisfactory explanation as to why the pillar has never rusted. A fence was erected around the pillar in 1997 in response to damage caused by visitors. There is a popular tradition that it was considered good luck if you could stand with your back to the pillar and make your hands meet behind it.

Ica Stones

Ica stones are considered by some people to be proof that there was once a technologically advanced civilization on Earth. They were reportedly discovered in a cave of unknown location near the city of Ica in Peru and popularized by Peruvian physician Javier Cabrera. Scientific testing of the more than fifteen thousand stones dates them as being from prehistoric times, but the stones are carved with images of things that would have been unfamiliar to any known prehistoric people. Contradicting both existing knowledge of Peruvian prehistory and evolution, they are considered prime examples of out-of-place artefacts. The stones are composed of andesite and vary in size from pebbles to boulders. They are shallowly engraved through their surface patina with a variety of images, purportedly depicting a variety of phenomena: For example, some of the stones seem to depict surgical equipment, blood transfusions, cesarean sections, and life support systems, as well as men using a telescope, Incan or Aztec men riding and attacking dinosaurs, extinct animals, flying machines, bestiality, star and land maps.

However, the circumstances of the stones' discovery are clouded. A farmer originally said that he had found them in a cave revealed when the Ica River changed its course, and indeed, the stones' composition shows that they could have come from the cave, near which archaeologists have found fossilized bones from prehistoric times. But when the Peruvian government arrested the farmer for selling some of the stones (because, under Peruvian law, as antiquities the stones would have belonged to the Peruvian government), he changed his story, saying that he had made the carvings himself. Skeptics accept this confession as the truth, while believers say that it was a lie told to keep the farmer from going to prison. Among those who believe that the stones were carved in prehistoric times, various theories have developed regarding the individuals who might have made them.

Peruvian researcher Javier Cabrera, who now owns many of the stones, believes that they were created by a prehistoric people, whom he calls Gliptolithic man, who were part of an advanced civilization with knowledge of space travel. He theorizes that these people left Earth at a time when the planet was undergoing changes that would have made it inhospitable, such as seismic cataclysms that split whole continents into pieces. Indeed, some Ica stones depict continents on Earth that do not exist. Others seem to show spacecraft hovering over the ground.

Interestingly, the cave where the farmer claimed to have found the stones is near an area of mysterious lines scratched into the ground, the Nazca lines, which some people claim was once a landing site for extraterrestrial spacecraft. Cabrera thinks that this is the site from which Gliptolithic man left Earth. He further believes, based on some of the celestial drawings on the stones, that the Gliptolithics headed for a planet in the Pleiades star cluster.

Hongshan Mysterious Artefacts

The Hongshan Culture was discovered in 1935 and covers an area from the Wuerjimulun River valley of Chifeng, Inner Mongolia in the north to Chaoyang, Lingyuan and the northern part of Hebei Province in the south, and extends eastward to cover Tongliao and Jinzhou. This Culture dates from 4500-2250 and is one of the earliest most advanced civilizations discovered to date in China. The Hongshan were temple builders and city builders who created some of the

earliest nephrite jade carvings. Their sophisticated Jade carving techniques employed technologies that exceeded simple explanations. Many of the Hongshan Jade artefacts are well persevered due to the fact that Hongshan culture utilized slab burial tombs and because of the dry arid climate of Inner Mongolia.

Perhaps the more famous known Hongshan Jade artefact is the Coiled Dragon Fetus. It has recently been discovered that the Hongshan possessed the knowledge of metallurgy and employed the use of copper (possible iron) metal tools to work their Jade masterpieces. Many Hongshan artefacts express the use of saw blades and drill instruments reflecting the fact that they were a highly technologically advanced civilization. Currently there is no known artefact evidence from other Neolithic cultures that show evidence of metal tools usage to shape jade during this very early period.

Recently Chinese archaeologists have discovered a Hongshan pyramid-shaped building dating back more than 5,000 years in the Inner Mongolia Autonomous Region, in north China. According to Guo Dashun, a renowned Chinese archaeologist, the "pyramid structure", located on a mountain ridge one kilometre north of Sijiazi Township in the Aohan Banner (county), is a three-storied stepped pyramid building that is 30 metres long and 15 metres wide. This discovery sheds light on the fact that these ancient people were one of the first known people to build pyramid structures. In addition, 7 tombs and a goddess temple were unearthed on the top of the "pyramid". There are many shattered statue pieces, including female head, shoulder, hands, breast pieces. The face of the goddess was painted with red colour, and her two eyes were embedded with green jade pieces. There are a lot of scattered pottery pieces with "mi (rice)" character carved on the inner wall of pottery. In addition, a palm-long male genital is also unearthed .

A unique characteristic of Hongshan culture is the coexistence of pottery and stone and jade ware. There are very diverse classes of jade ware, which have different sizes from small ornament to huge ritual ware and can have usage in every aspect of the social functions. Hongshan culture jade article can be categorized into five classes: tool class, such as axe, spin, rod, etc.; ornament class, such as ring, bracelet, pin, tube, etc.; ritual ware class, such as bell, battel-axe, sei-annular pendant, Pei, etc; animal class, such as dragon, pig dragon, bird, turtle, silkworm, etc.; and statue class. The most representative pieces are "C"-shaped dragon and pig dragon. The manufacturing process of Hongshan jade articles utilized mill and polishing technique, such that there is no carving marks on the jade articles.

The processing technique of Hongshan culture is quite different from that of Liangzhu culture. It was a general belief of Chinese archeologist that the process of Liangzhu Jade articles utilized teeth from shark, agate, and crystal. Japanese archaeologist think diamond was used for processing. These very early Neolithic Hongshan people were transient living in a region that falls between steppe and

91

agricultural climate zones. In the middle period of Hongshan culture it becomes evident that a husbandry and agricultural based society emerges that leads to advancement in social structure.

Discoveries from Hongshan burial sites show that they had class structure and interesting is the fact that they cultivated millet and did not grow rice. Animal husbandry appears to have been highly advanced with the domestication of pigs and ducks. There is existing Jade artefact evidence that points to the possibility that they were one of the earliest people to domestic the horse. Archeological evidence shows that with the emergence of social stratification and a ruling class a large handicraft industry of jade workers flourished.

Hongshan Jade ritual and art objects were created for a period of more than 2,000 years. Contrary to what Western arm chair archaeologist have stated, Hongshan jades have been discovered in large quantities with over 52 different types of Jade objects in various shapes and forms. The most remarkable discoveries have been very recent in areas that are much further south of where the Hongshan Civilization was thought to have been centreed.

Recent finds from a tomb at Niuheliang and two smaller mound tombs excavated in the same area were the discoveries of metal-casting technologies that were disclosed by small copper rings unearthed at these sites. The use of kilns to produce highly advanced painted and non painted pottery gave the Hongshan the power of intense heat to explore metallurgy.

According to Wong Tien Chung, these ancient people extracted iron ore/nickel alloys from meteorites to make ritual jade shaping tools. In the first place, archeological studies show that Hongshan Culture was developed on the basis of Xinglongwa Culture and Zhaobaogou Culture, and the inheritance and development in religious traditions between the three cultures are evident. No sites devoted exclusively to sacrificial rites have been found so far in Xinglongwa Culture and Zhaobaogou Culture. The discovery of Niuheliang Relics in the 1970s indicates that large-scaled centres for sacrificial rites had shown up by the end of Hongshan Culture. This is not only a breakthrough in the study of Hongshan Culture, but a discovery of great significance to the exploration of the origin of the Chinese civilization. Secondly, Hongshan Culture is credited with remarkable achievements in architecture, pottery-making, jade-carving and pottery sculptures which are at higher levels than those of Xinglongwa Culture and Zhaobaogou Culture. The duet of square pottery molds unearthed at the relics of a house of Hongshan Culture at Xitai, Aohan Banner, which is the earliest mold for metal casting, shows that the early people of Hongshan Culture had mastered the technology of bronze casting.

Based on artefact evidence and 30 years of study that the Hongshan employed advanced jade shaping and carving tools that may have been made from meteorite iron. One fascinating study is the evidence of high content iron found in black jades used for ritual objects by the early Hongshan. Many of these artefacts are magnetic and express the possibility that the Hongshan were aware of magnetic earth forces.

Another fascinating observation through the study of Hongshan jade artefacts is the abundance of "Alien" like motifs and figurines that completely unexplainable as they are not found in other Neolithic Cultures. It is obvious from the study of Hongshan artefacts that a highly sophisticated knowledge of mathematics and Astronomy become evident. The extensive employment of ritual jades in China by the Hongshan during its late prehistory must certainly demonstrate to the world of archeology that these people were not "Neolithic Age" but rather "Jade Age" people. More great discoveries wait under the earth of China. The Hongshan were actually the Xinglongwa people who migrated into China from Mongolia when global weather conditions turned their rich forested world into desert.

Recent discoveries reveal that the Xinglongwa people had sophisticated jade carving techniques over 8,500 years ago! Archeologists believe that the discovery of these relics, as well as of the pyramid itself, will be crucial in learning more about both the spiritual and earthbound life of the peoples of the Hongshan culture. The long lost historic trails of these great people who were called the Hongshan are waiting to be discovered. The greatest discoveries of the origins of human civilization await us in China. Perhaps, it may be discovered that they are indeed descendents from a long lost advanced civilization.

Hemet Maze Stone

A gray boulder emblazoned with the intricate design of a labyrinthine maze enclosed in a 3 1/2-foot square. The petroglyph is located on a mountainside just west of Hemet, California, some 90 miles southeast of Los Angeles. Accumulation on its surface of a light patina known locally as "desert varnish" suggests the incised carving was executed between 3,000 and 4,000 years ago, despite the insistence of mainstream archaeologists, who insist, on tenuous physical evidence, that it could be no more than a few centuries old. About 50 maze-stones have been identified throughout California, in Orange, Riverside, Imperial, and San Diego counties, and at least 14 examples of labyrinthine rock art are known in the remote area of Palm Springs. All of them have been found within 150 miles of each other, and virtually every one is rectangular, although varying in size from 4 inches to several feet in diametre. They are invariably located on boulder-strewn mountainsides, and are perhaps the remnants of a pilgrimage route dedicated to commemorating a seminal event in the deep past.

The maze itself is in the form of a swastika, a sacred symbol for numerous Native American tribes across the continent. Among the Hopi Indians, the hooked cross signifies the migration of their tribe from the east following a great flood that overwhelmed early mankind.

Although it is not known if Hopi forefathers carved the Hemet Maze Stone, the Atlantean significance of their ancestral myth is suggested by its westward oriented design. These implications are complimented by a late 15th-century example of Mexican featherwork in a similar, swastika-like design (with reversed orientation, however) belonging to a transparently Atlantean figure in Mesoamerican myth, Chalchiuhtlicue; "Our Lady of the Turquoise Skirt" was the Aztec goddess of death at sea. Hopi sand paintings, spiritual devices for the removal of illness, are often formed into swastikas, with the patient made to sit at its centre. In the bottom-left corner of the square outline of the Hemet Maze Stone is a simple, much smaller, reversed, or right-oriented hooked cross, known in Buddhism as the sauvastika.

Both swastikas and sauvastikas are common images throughout Asia, where they denote Buddha's right and left foot, respectively, and refer to his missionary travels throughout the world. As such, the Buddhist swastika-sauvastika and California petroglyph appear to share a parallel symbolism which both Asians and ancient Americans may have received independently from a common source. James Churchward, a 20th-century authority on Mu, stated that the swastika was the Pacific civilization's foremost emblem. He referred to it as "the key of universal movement," a characterization complimenting both Hopi and Buddhist symbolism. The questions remains : what the purpose of this stone, and who build it? Is it Atlantean?

Saqqara Bird

The Saqqara Bird is a bird-like artefact made of sycamore wood, discovered during the 1891 excavation of the Pa-di-Imen tomb in Saqqara, Egypt. It dates back to at least 200 BC and is now housed in the Egyptian Museum in Cairo. It has a wingspan of 7.2 inches and weighs 39.120 grams. The artefact has a beak, no holes for feathers, and one eye, and was painted to resemble a falcon without clear images and carving of feathers on the wings. Perhaps the most intriguing speculation is that the "Bird" may show that an understanding of the principles of aviation existed many centuries before such are generally believed to have first been discovered. The Ancient Egyptians had knowledge to some extent of sail construction. Since the 5.6-inch long object closely resembles a model airplane, it has led one Egyptologist, Khalil Messiha, and others to speculate that the Ancient Egyptians developed the first aircraft. Messiha, who was the first to argue that the model did not represent a bird, wrote in 1983 that it "represents a diminutive of an original monoplane still present in Saqqara."

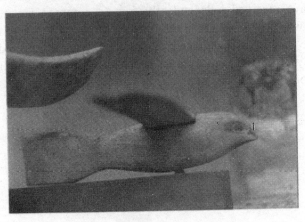

Hadji Ahmed Map

It is dated 1559 and it shows the entire world in a somewhat fanciful type of projection that is more art than science and which was typical of Arab chartwork of the time. More amazingly, it shows a land bridge between Siberia and Alaska. There are some "extra" islands that do not presently exist, but these islands did exist ten thousand years ago, near the end of the Ice Age when the sea level was exactly 200-300 feet lower than today – indicating how ancient the source map must be. The Hadji Ahmed Map was drawn by an Arab geographer from Damascus, only obscurely known to history. A careful look will show that Hadji Ahmed "improved" the Mediterranean according to Ptolemy, and thus distorted it, and also drew Africa according to the best Portuguese information that he could get, and distorted Africa too in a manner completely typical of the time.

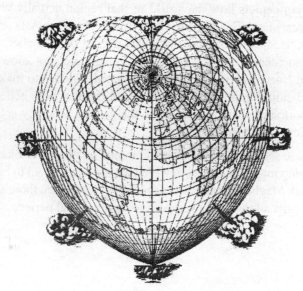

But when we look at North America and South America we see an almost modern shape that could compare well with Mercator's Map of South America drawn 10 years later from contemporary explorers' information. Thankfully, Hadji Ahmed apparently had no access to contemporary maps and charts of the Americas and so was stuck with simply copying some mysterious mappamundi in his possession.

This unknown source map of Hadji Ahmed was more accurate than the best information available in 1559 and so the map looks very modern. It shows Baja, California, which had not been mapped then. It shows the Northwest Coast of North America, including Alaska, which had not been discovered then. It shows the Hawaiian Islands in the Pacific, which were not discovered until two hundred years later. It shows a sprinkling of islands in the Pacific, a sort of vague and suggestive rendition of the Polynesian Islands, but they had not been discovered yet. It shows Antarctica clearly, and even a suggestion of the Palmer Peninsula, and that had not been discovered then either.

The Far East, insofar as it can be made out in the curious "splitapple" projection used in the map, is distorted but reasonably accurate. But the strange and unnerving thing is the region of Alaska and Asia. The curve of the Aleutian Islands is depicted accurately, but there is no Bering Strait and the whole area is land. This part of the map depicts how the world of that region actually was – but 10,000 years ago! The "Bering Land Bridge" between Asia and North America, is shown correctly. This fact almost defies belief. Or, is it just a coincidence? Perhaps a mediocre mapmaker, not knowing how Asia and North America actually terminated, decided to make things easy and simply join them. Hapgood and Bradley both believed that all the portolans share a peculiarity: the general accuracy is there but the sea level seems too low.

These sea-level problems are common to all the portolans and to the existing mappamundi from which the portolans seem to have been excerpted. Maybe the earth was accurately mapped ten thousand years ago, and that a few copies survived to the medieval period.

The Glozel Artefacts

In Glozel, France, there is a little necropolis where over 60 years ago finds have been made. About 2500 objects have been discovered with carved symbols, animals and mysterious inscriptions. On almost every object made of bones or ceramic there is script. Most of the artefacts were dated 3000 B. C. But there are also pieces that are younger and some that might be 17.000 years old. Less known is the fact that also numerous stone relics with carvings were found, that are very old and caused controversy among the French scientists. The artefacts were dated between 4.500 and 15.000 years. Also some tablets of clay with different unknown letters have been found. This discovery wasn't taken seriously because the scientists wouldn't believe that men of the Ice Age were able to make such objects. The typical carvings of Glozel are also found on stone relics. The meaning of those findings is unknown. Experts think that they might have been used for an occult purpose or for ceremonies.

The main problem with the collection of Glozel is, that something similar wasn't found yet. But the symbols on the tablets are similar to symbols of the Harappa culture. In April 1999 the finds have been analysed by archaeologists from the Harvard University – they have been proven as authentically ancient pieces. The discovery was made on 1 March 1924 by 17-year-old Émile Fradin (born August 8, 1906) and his grandfather Claude Fradin. Émile was guiding a cow-drawn plow when its foot became stuck in a cavity. Freeing the cow, the Fradins uncovered an underground chamber, with walls of clay bricks and 16 clay floor tiles, containing human bones and ceramic fragments. Adrienne Picandet, a local teacher, visited the Fradins' farm in March, and afterwards informed the Minister of Education about the site. On July 9, another teacher, Benoit Clément, visited the Fradins representing the Société d'Émulation du Bourbonnais, later returning with a man called Viple. Clément and Viple used pickaxes to break down the chamber's remaining walls, which they took away with them. Later,

Viple wrote to Émile Fradin identifying the site as Gallo-Roman, dating to between about A.D 100-400, and possibly of archeological importance. Antonin Morlet, a Vichy physician and amateur archaeologist, visited the farm on 26 April, offering 200 francs to be allowed to complete the excavation. Morlet began his excavations on 24 May, 1925, discovering tablets, bisexual idols, bone and flint tools, engraved stones and a few human bones continued to appear from the soil. He also found, in the top layer of soil, a few pieces of stoneware pottery and some vitrified objects. Below that was a layer of yellowish clayey colluvium, in which most of the older artefacts were found. Some 100 ceramic tablets bearing inscriptions are among the artefacts found at Glozel. The inscriptions are, on average, on six or seven lines, mostly on a single side, although some specimens are inscribed on both faces.

When Dr. Capitan, an elderly and very famous French archaeologist, visited Vichy for his health, Dr. Morlet invited him to visit the site. Capitan was enthusiastic and offered to publish information on the finds at Glozel. But Dr. Morlet, becoming alarmed at indications that Capitan wished to appropriate the site for himself, hastily published the first of a series of little booklets on Glozel.

Morlet identified the site as Neolithic in a report entitled Nouvelle Station Néolithique published in September 1925, with Émile Fradin listed as co-author. French archaeologists were quick to point out the improbability of Morlet's interpretation of the site. They were also outraged that an amateur archaeologist and a young peasant boy had the presumption to publish books about Glozel. Capitan changed his mind about the authenticity of the finds. And so the controversy began.

Two other tombs were uncovered in 1927. More excavations were performed in April 1928. After 1941, a new law outlawed private excavations, and the site remained untouched until the Ministry of Culture re-opened excavations in 1983. The full report was never published, but a 13-page summary appeared in 1995. The authors suggest that the site is medieval (roughly A.D. 500 – 1500), possibly containing some earlier Iron Age objects, but was likely enriched by forgeries.

However in March 2001 there was an examination and analysis of the artefacts. It resulted that the objects haven't been worked with a metal tool. The pictured animals and the symbols have been made with the same types of tools. That means that the script has not been added later, like sceptics are used to say.

The symbols on the tablets are reminiscent of the Phoenician alphabet, but they have not been conclusively deciphered. There were numerous claims of decypherment, including identification of the language of the inscriptions as Basque, Chaldean, Eteocretan, Hebrew, Iberian, Latin, Berber, Ligurian, Phoenician and Turkic.

Giant Stone Eggs

Mysterious giant "stone eggs" discovered on 2007 at a construction site in Bandeng Hill and Zhanlong Hill, Gongxi Town of Hunan Province. According to The Epoch Times, the "eggs," along with a large copper sword, were unearthed by highway construction workers while they were digging the foundation for a road. Some geologists

have speculated the eggs are natural formations of carbonate rock which snowballed slowly in oscillating water, but no one is certain what they are, indeed, they are natural. The unique perfection of their shape suggests to some that they are of intelligent design.

Ranging from watermelon – to table-size, the eggs have been taken from many "nests" uncovered by the workers. The eggs are oval in shape, with a wide range of sizes; the smallest one being no bigger than a water melon, while the largest is reported as being the size of a big table. Upon closer examination they look like eggs from the outside, but are very shiny and black on the inside. The copper sword which the construction team had also discovered was found to weigh over 1,000 pounds. Unfortunately the sword disappeared later and there are no leads as to the identities of the people involved in the theft. The incident has been reported to the police.

The Chinese "eggs" remind some observers of the large and perfectly spherical stone balls found in many places in Costa Rica. Anthropologist George Erikson and his colleague Ivar Zapp in their book Atlantis in America: Navigators of the Ancient World argued that the mysterious Costa Rican balls are markers from a lost ancient navigation system. So far, though, no one has offered any such theory for the Chinese finds.

Genetic Disk

This disk from South America is one of the most interesting and confusing finds of archaeology. The unique relic is made of black stone and measures about 22 cm in diametre. It weights about 2 kg. It was not made of artificial materials like cement but of lydite. It was dated in a prehistoric epoch, and assigned to the Muisca-culture. On the disk there are carvings that describes the astonishing knowledge of our ancestors. The object has been examined in the Museum of Natural History, Vienna, Austria. Dr. Vera M. F. Hammer, expert for precious stones and minerals, analysed the object.

The symbols on the disk are very impressive. The obverse and reverse side are decorated with carvings and ornaments, separated with single vertical stripes. On the edge of the disk there is a symbol of a snake. In the middle the disk shows a hole, maybe a hint that the disc originally was fixed on a stick and then turned around. One side shows biological details like male sperms, female egg cell and the genitals, the fertilized egg, foetus and the growing embryo. The other side shows scenes that could be interpreted as the cell division and depiction of frog creatures in different stages.

Dr. Algund Eemboom MD, and his colleges analysed the different segments of the disk. His result was that it is possible to recognize the phases of evolution of human life on the disk. Very significant are the distant lying eyes and the broad nose. This is a characteristic of the embryonic structure of the head.

Prof. Dr. Rudolf Distelberger, internationally recognized expert for precious stones and director of the Schatzkammer, Vienna, said that the disk has a very complex content. That is the reason why many scientists cried fraud as the disk appeared. It cannot be classified in the known South American system of cultures.

Galley Hill Skeleton

In 1888, workmen removing deposits at Galley Hill, near London, England, exposed a bed of chalk. The overlying layers of sand, loam, and gravel were about 10 or 11 feet thick. One workman, Jack Allsop, informed Robert Elliott, a collector of prehistoric items, that he had discovered a human skeleton firmly embedded in these deposits about 8 feet below the surface and about 2 feet above the chalk bed. According to modern opinion, the Galley Hill site would date to the Holstein interglacial, which occurred about 330,000 years ago. Anatomically, the Galley Hill skeleton was judged to be of the modern human type. Most scientists now think that anatomically modern humans (Homo sapiens sapiens) originated in Africa around 100,000 years ago. They say that Homo sapiens sapiens eventually entered Europe in the form of Cro-Magnon man approximately 30,000 years ago, replacing the Neanderthals. Just what do modern paleoanthropologists say about the Galley Hill skeleton?

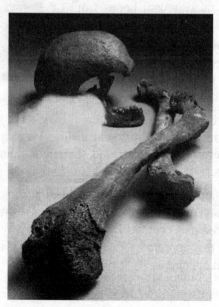

Allsop had removed the skull but left the rest of the skeleton in place. Elliott stated that he saw the skeleton firmly embedded in the stratum: "We carefully looked for any signs of the section being disturbed, but failed: the stratification being unbroken." Elliott then removed the skeleton and later gave it to E. T. Newton, who published a report granting it great age. A schoolmaster named M. H. Heys observed the bones in the apparently undisturbed deposits before Elliott removed the skeleton. Heys also saw the skull just after it was exposed by a workman excavating the deposits. Heys said about the bones: "No doubt could possibly arise to the observation of an ordinary intelligent person of their deposition contemporaneously with that of the gravel. . . . This undisturbed state of the stratum was so palpable to the workman that he said, 'The man or animal was not buried by anybody.'"

Numerous stone tools were also recovered from the Galley Hill site. Despite the stratigraphic evidence reported by Heys and Elliott, K. P. Oakley and M. F. A. Montagu concluded in 1949 that the skeleton must have been recently buried in the Middle Pleistocene deposits. They considered the bones, which were not fossilized, to be only a few thousand years old. This is also the opinion of almost all anthropologists today. The Galley Hill bones had a nitrogen content similar to that of fairly recent bones from other sites in England. Nitrogen is one of the constituent elements of protein, which normally decays with the passage of time. But there are many recorded cases of proteins being preserved in fossils for millions of years. Because the degree of nitrogen preservation may vary from site to site, one cannot say for certain that the relatively high nitrogen content of the Galley Hill bones means they are recent.

The Galley Hill bones were found in loam, a clayey sediment known to preserve protein. Oakley and Montagu found the Galley Hill human bones had a fluorine content similar to that of Late Pleistocene and Holocene (recent) bones from other sites. It is known that bones absorb fluorine from groundwater. But the fluorine content of groundwater may vary widely from place to place and this makes comparison of fluorine contents of bones from different sites an unreliable indicator of their relative ages. Later, the British Museum Research Laboratory obtained a carbon 14 date of 3,310 years for the Galley Hill skeleton. But this test was performed using methods now considered unreliable. Also, it is highly probable that the Galley Hill bones, kept in a museum for 80 years, were contaminated with recent carbon, causing the test to give a falsely young date.

In attempting to discredit the testimony of Elliott and Heys, who said no signs of burial were evident at Galley Hill, Oakley and Montagu offered several arguments in addition to their chemical and radiometric tests. For example, Oakley and Montagu argued that the relatively complete nature of the Galley Hill skeleton was a sure sign that it was deliberately buried. In fact, almost all of the ribs, the backbone, the forearms, hands, and feet were missing. In the case of Lucy, the most famous specimen of Australopithecus afarensis, more of the skeleton was preserved. And no one has yet suggested that australopithecines buried their dead. Scientists have also discovered fairly complete skeletal remains of Homo erectus and Homo habilis individuals. These cases, as all paleoanthropologists would agree, definitely do not involve deliberate burial. It is thus possible for relatively complete hominid skeletons to be preserved apart from burial. But even if the Galley Hill skeleton was a burial, the burial may not have been recent.

Sir Arthur Keith suggested in 1928: "Weighing all the evidence, we are forced to the conclusion that the Galley Hill skeleton represents a man. . . . buried when the lower gravel formed a land surface." As can be seen, old bones point beyond themselves, quite obliquely, to events in the remote and inaccessible past. Controversy about their age is almost certain to arise, and in many cases the available evidence is insufficient to allow disputes to be definitely settled. This would appear to be true of Galley Hill. The report of Oakley and Montagu casts doubt on the testimony of Elliott and Heys. At the same time, the testimony of Elliott and Heys casts doubt on the report of Oakley and Montagu.

Dogu Statues

The Dogu statues crafted by the Jomon people of Japan and dated to about 5000 BC have an oddly mechanical appearance. It tend to have large faces, small arms and hands and compact bodies. Some appear to wear goggles or have "heart-shaped" faces. Most have marks on the face, chest and shoulders, which suggest tattooing and probable incision with bamboo. Dogu first appeared in early Jomon but began to flourish in Middle Jomon through Late Jomon and were found all over Japan with northern Japan, the Tohoku region, yielding the most variety. Archaeologists are baffled by these statues because they resemble no other objects on earth.

As for Jomon pottery, Dogu has various styles by exhumation area and generation. According to the National Museum of Japanese

History, the total number found throughout Japan is approximately 15,000. Most of the Dogu have been found in East Japan and it is rare to find one in West Japan. Now they can be found in the Japan Archaeological Collection of Tohoku University, Sendai and several museum in Japan.

Although huge numbers of Dogu statues were dug up by archaeologist in various stages of "detail" but many were found broken, and seemingly on purpose. Unbroken figures are rare, and most are missing an arm, leg or other body part. In many cases, the parts have been cut off. The purpose of the Dogu remains unclear but, most likely, the Dogu acted as effigies of people, that manifested some kind of sympathetic magic. There are many theories on what they were used for with the main agreement being they were a talisman for good health or safe childbirth. As many were excavated in fragments, it's believed that after the wish was fulfilled, or not, the dogu was broken and thrown on the trash heap; that's where many were discovered. Another theory is that these were goddesses to whom Jomon people prayed to for food and health. Other explanations are toys for children, funerary offerings, or objects used in some unknown ritual. And, of course, there are those who believe they were aliens from outer space as ancient astronauts. While Vaughn M. Greene in his books "*Astronauts of Ancient Japan and The Six Thousand Year Old Space Suit*", argues that these statues are actually space suits worn by extraterrestrials who visited earth thousands of years ago.

Dogu statues are totally unique. There are no other figures exactly like them in the ancient world. In several years of research, archaeologists have found indications that these same ancient astronauts were seen all over the world. The 7,000-year-old drawings at Val Cominica, Italy, the prehistoric Tassali, Sahara, and ancient Australian Aborigine sketches all show helmeted, suited-up figures. There are statues, such as the Tula giants in Mexico, the Tiahuanaco space gods in Bolivia, the Cro-Magnon Venus cult of Europe, which show similar features. Figurines of the 8,000-year-old Mohenjo Daro culture in India are almost identical.

Dendera Light

The Dendera light comprises three stone reliefs (one single and a double representation) in the Hathor temple at the Dendera Temple complex located in Egypt. The images are interpreted by traditional Egyptologists to depicting lotus flowers spawning a snake, representing aspects of Egyptian mythology. Controversy arose when the main object in the images was interpreted by some as electric lamps based on comparison to modern devices. These individuals believe the object may be electric lamps. Engineers have constructed a working model based on the reliefs and some authors (such as Peter Krassa and Reinhard Habeck) have produced a basic theory of the device's operation.

The Dropa Stones

There have been many unusual and puzzling artefacts that have been unearthed, or otherwise discovered, that do not fit into conventional theories of our geologic and historical past, one of them is the Dropa Stones. The "stones" were found buried beneath millennia of dust in 1938 on an archeological expedition led by Dr. Chi Pu Tei in caves in the Baian-Kara-Ula mountains on the border that divides China and Tibet. Chi Pu Tei, a professor of archaeology at Beijing University, was leading some his students on an expedition to survey a series of interlinking caves in the Himalayan mountains. According to one account, the caves may have been artificially carved, and were more like a complex system of tunnels and underground storerooms. The walls were squared and glazed, as if cut into the mountain with a source of extreme heat.

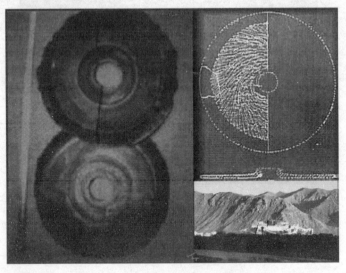

Inside the caves they found several ancient, and neatly arranged burial sites, and in them the skeletal remains of a strange creatures. The skeletons had abnormally big heads, with small, thin, fragile bodies.

A member of the team suggested that these might be the remains of an unknown species of mountain gorilla.

There were no epitaphs at the graves, but instead numbering several hundred stones in all were found, each disk measured about nine inches in diametre having 3/4 inch wide holes in their centres, and spiral grooves etched into the surface, like an ancient phonograph record. On the walls were carved pictures of the rising sun, moon, stars, the land, mountains, and lines of pea-sized dots connecting the earth with the sky. The cave drawings had been determined to be about 12,000 years old and the artefacts found with the stone disks have been dated to about 10,000 to 12,000 years old.

Small hieroglyphics were found in the grooves that, when translated, tell of an extraordinary story of extraterrestrials, who called themselves the Dropa, who had crash-landed in the mountains of China. Reports indicate that, in some of the caves, along with the disks, were discovered the remains of the Dropa, or their descendents, and that they may have, in fact, been Chinese.

proved the single biggest haul of artefacts with 15,000 fragments of 500 different manuscripts.

The Dead Sea Scrolls

The northern shore of the Dead Sea is a particularly dry, arid place. It is 13 miles from Jerusalem, and even though the area is often shrouded in haze, the humidity levels are extremely low: it is the perfect place to preserve ancient artefacts. In the spring of 1947 two young Bedouin shepherds were looking for a lost goat among the cliffs in the area known as Qumran. As they hunted from cave to cave, they came upon a store of jars containing many papyrus and parchment manuscripts. These scrolls only came to prominence later that year when the Bedouin sold seven of the texts to a local antiquities dealer. As the academic world grew to hear about the discoveries, intense excitement burst through the global community of historians. Little did they know that this would be the most important discovery of ancient scrolls in the entire century. In 1949 the exact location of the initial find was discovered, and the cave was given a thorough archaeological survey. More fragments of scrolls were uncovered, along with pieces of cloth, pottery and wood.

Over the next seven years ten more caves containing ancient texts were found in the Qumran area, and the remains of around 850 different scrolls were discovered in total. The caves were named in the order that they were searched, and cave four, uncovered in 1952, proved the single biggest haul of artefacts with 15,000 fragments of 500 different manuscripts.

A complex of ancient structures close to the caves, referred to as the Qumran ruin, was also excavated. What the scientists discovered was that the scrolls and the ruin both dated from between the third century BC and 68 AD, placing them around the time of Christ. It seems the texts formed the library of a Jewish sect, similar to the Essenes. The Essenes were a strict Torah observing society, who disliked the established priesthood and may have actually been wiped out by the Jerusalem based church. It is thought the ruins at Qumran formed part of their society, and the scrolls were hidden from the advancing Roman army around AD 70. The truly fascinating thing about the scrolls is not so much their history, but what they actually say. The scrolls have been deciphered and reconstructed by expert modern scholars. They tend to fall into two groups: texts concerned with religion and others revealing details of daily lives and history. There are copies of many biblical writings, and all but one book of the Old Testament. More interestingly, there are previously unseen psalms authored by King David and Joshua, and also some prophecies attributed to Ezekiel, Jeremiah and Daniel that do not appear in the Bible. The scrolls contain previously unknown stories about Enoch, Abraham and Noah. Similarly the lost words of Amram, Joseph, Judah, Levi and Naphtali are also revealed in the texts. Surprisingly, given their date and proximity to New Testament events, the life of Jesus Christ is not mentioned. The scrolls are mainly written in Hebrew, but also feature passages in Aramaic and Greek.

Some scrolls explain laws and codes of battle, whereas others recount poems and the philosophies of wise men. The most enigmatic information contained in the scrolls lists 64 places around Israel where ancient treasures are buried. It is suggested that not only gold and silver is hidden there, but many of the holy objects from the temple of Jerusalem were also deposited in distant, unknown places for safekeeping. Although the scrolls were all discovered within eight years, the collection was scattered among universities, museums and scholarly institutions across the world.

Da Vinci's Mysterious Robot

Around the year A.D. 1495, Leonardo da Vinci designed (and perhaps even built) a mechanical armoured knight, probably the first humanoid robot in history. The machinery inside da Vinci's robot, a cable-and-pulley-driven artificial man was designed to create the illusion that a real person was inside. This robot could sit up, wave its arms, and move its head while opening and closing an anatomically correct jaw. It may even have emitted sounds to the accompaniment of automated musical instruments, such as drums. The design notes for the robot appear in sketchbooks that were rediscovered in the 1950s. It is not known whether or not an attempt was made to build the device. In fact, there were quite a few inventors in medieval times who built machines similar to this to entertain royalty. Da Vinci's robot was dressed in a typical, late-15th century German-Italian suits of armour. From da Vinci's designs, it appears that all the joints moved in unison, powered and controlled by a mechanical, analogue-programable controller located within the chest. The legs were powered separately by an external crank assembly driving the cable, which was connected to important locations in the ankle, knee, and hip.

One of the scientist that very interested with da Vinci's Robot is Mark Elling Rosheim, a roboticist who has produced designs for NASA and Lockheed Martin. He is not simply interested in studying da Vinci, but that he would like to be da Vinci. There are certain parallels. Da Vinci was self-taught and often referred to himself as an omo sanze lettere – a man without letters; Rosheim is a high school dropout. Da Vinci was apprenticed to Andrea del Verrocchio's workshop at age 15; Rosheim filed for his first patent – for a hydraulically powered servomechanism – at age 18. Da Vinci was determined to understand the architecture of the human body. By the time he was 65, he had dissected the corpses of more than 30 men and women of all ages. Rosheim is a student of kinesiology who has paid particular attention to the human wrist. In a basement workshop, he create a prototype of his Omniwrist, a joint that can move in any direction across a full hemisphere, without gears.

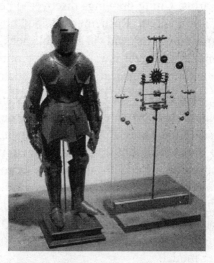

In the early 1990s, Rosheim's twin passions of da Vinci and robotics fatefully converged. After an Italian scholar showed Rosheim some recently recovered da Vinci drawings, Rosheim took a fresh look at what had been dubbed "Leonardo's automobile," a wooden three-wheeled cart. Da Vinci enthusiasts have reconstructed the automobile several times during the past century, but it's never worked. The device seemed destined to join the ranks of da Vinci's grandiose but flawed inventions – what one scholar called his "impossible machines." To Rosheim, the machine was hardly impossible. Immersing himself in the minutiae of each sketch, gleaning inspiration from inventions that came later, he concluded that the device was not simply a spring-powered cart – as novel as that might be for 1478 – but something more radically innovative. Da Vinci's automobile, Rosheim maintains, is actually a robot with its own set of programmable instructions. This "precursor to mobile robots," Rosheim suggests, might even be "the first record of a programmable analog computer in the history of civilization."

The notion that da Vinci was some sort of proto-computer geek is not as far-fetched as it sounds. In a 1996 article in the journal Achademia Leonardi Vinci, Rosheim offered compelling historical and mechanical evidence that da Vinci had designed – and perhaps built

- automata. Rosheim pointed to da Vinci's so-called Robot Knight, a cable-and-pulley-driven artificial man, which had been thought to be a simple suit of arms. Citing drawings discovered decades earlier by Italian scholar Carlo Pedretti, Rosheim explained how the figure "sat up, waved its arms, moved its head via a flexible neck, and opened and closed its anatomically correct jaw - possibly emitting sound while accompanied by automated musical instruments such as drums."

The robot, the theory goes, may have been commissioned by the Sforza rulers as court entertainment or an exhibit in a kind of mechanical sculpture garden. A finished drawing of the knight has never been recovered, but Rosheim, armed with mechanical aptitude and a strong knowledge of the history of robotics, was able to extrapolate its use from a patchwork of drawings. Paolo Galluzzi, director of Florence's Institute and Museum of the History of Science, described Rosheim's robot thesis as "absolutely convincing." Galluzzi included the knight in an exhibition and commissioned Rosheim to create a computer model.

In 2002, Rosheim was invited by the BBC to build a prototype. His model was able to walk and wave – proving Rosheim's theory once and for all. Vindicated, Rosheim revisited other da Vinci machines. His searching led to a 1975 article written by Pedretti, the same scholar who had done pivotal research on the knight. The article presented Pedretti's analysis of a new sheet of drawings discovered in a collection at Florence's Uffizi. They were sketched by an anonymous 16th-century draftsman but included copies of da Vinci's technological studies. Pedretti focused on one sketch that clearly outlined the function of the arbalest-like springs in the depiction of da Vinci's baffling three-wheeled cart. They were, he realized, not for power, as earlier scholars had thought, but for steering.

Like an escapement mechanism for clocks, the springs retained movement but didn't generate it. He concluded that the movement must come from somewhere else. So Pedretti looked back at da Vinci's original drawing and noticed a faint circle in the centre of one of the car's toothed gears. The little circle, he believed, was almost a suggestion to look for something transparent, something beneath the cart. Perhaps there were larger coil springs, hidden inside the tambours, that would drive the cart. The sketch of the cart is not particularly impressive to look at. On the top of the page is a crudely drawn wagon with some sort of gear mechanism.

The bulk of the page is dominated by a closer view of that mechanism, which combines a crossbow-like arbalest with the grooved gears and verge-and-foliot apparatus found in medieval clocks. On the periphery of the page, as on many Codex pages, there are details of component parts. Though Pedretti had uncovered fragments of robot designs in da Vinci's sketchbooks, he couldn't figure out how they fit together. Rosheim, who had started corresponding with Pedretti after meeting him in 1993, began developing a CAD reconstruction and faxing documents to Pedretti at night. It was like a fill-in-the-blanks puzzle. "There's nothing saying, This is an automaton," Rosheim recalls, explaining how he contrived a robot. "I'm working with napkin sketches. It's very fragmentary stuff – otherwise it would have been done centuries ago."

To divine what the artist envisioned for the cart's undercarriage, Rosheim tried to internalize the da Vinci method, studying myriad other drawings "to load it up into my subconscious" and inventing "an internal calculus to try and figure out everything." One of the biggest breakthroughs, strangely enough, came not from da Vinci's own work but from a drawing Rosheim had of a karakuri, an 18th-century Japanese tea-carrying automaton (often resembling a geisha) – the Sony Qrio of shogunate Japan. The movement of the karakuri was determined by the placement of cams, small appendages on a wheel or shaft that engage a lever and convert rotary power to linear power. (Cams are still found in today's car engines.)

Looking at the karakuri, Rosheim thought that da Vinci's cart might contain a similar arrangement. Sure enough, he found small camlike protrusions attached to one of the toothed wheels in da Vinci's drawing. The karakuri seemed to provide the missing link to understanding the cart's undercarriage – a perspective not shown in the sketches. Rosheim's epiphany answered questions he'd been unable to resolve: How did the escapement work? How did you regulate the speed – in other words, the clock of the computer? How did that connect to the rest of the drivetrain? Once you understand the cams, the faint circles underneath the middle of the frame of the perspective view suddenly make sense, he says. "Obviously, they connect to one of those levers that's cam-controlled."

The inspiration may have come from 18th-century Japan, but Rosheim says his ideas – unlike previous reconstructions – mesh perfectly with da Vinci's original design. So here you had a small, front-wheel-drive cart no more than 20 inches square – many Codex illustrations are one-to-one scale fabrication drawings – that could, on the basis of spring-loaded power, be triggered via remote control and run a specific course, turning in a programmed direction at a certain point and perhaps even executing a "special effect" or two. What on earth was it for? If Rosheim was able to supply the how of da Vinci's robot cart, Pedretti could offer a why: court entertainment. Da Vinci, he says, would have been 26 when he built the cart.

It was 1478, and Florence was especially volatile: The Pazzis were conspiring against the reigning Medici family (Da Vinci sketched the hanged Bernardo Bandini, who murdered Giuliano de Medici during the plot). The historical record offers no mention of da Vinci having built a cart. Pedretti, however, unearthed a potential clue. "I found a fantastic document, date 1600," Pedretti says. "It's a description of a banquet held in Paris to honour the new queen of France, who was a Medici. On that occasion, Michelangelo Buonarroti the Younger observed the presentation of a mechanical lion. It walked, opened its chest, and in place of a heart it had fleurs-de-lis." Pedretti pauses, gathering more papers. "This document, which was totally unknown, says this was a concept similar to one that Leonardo carried out in Lyons on the occasion of Francis I."

It appears da Vinci had engaged in high tech diplomacy circa 1515. The cart, suggests Pedretti, may have been an early study in an emerging da Vinci sideline. Leonardo, he believes, created animated spectacles centuries before the great age of the European automata of Jacques de Vaucansan and Wolfgang von Kempelen. "The irony of the whole thing is that there is not a single hint in Leonardo's manuscripts of this greatest technological invention," Pedretti says. "Imagine to have a lion walk and stand on its legs and open up its chest – this is top

118

technology!" What happened to those pages of drawings that would have revealed the inner workings of these wondrous devices? Perhaps they lie misfiled in some lost archive; perhaps they were destroyed by some church authority in the manner of Albertus Magnus's mechanical woman, smashed by Thomas Aquinas as a work of the devil.

Half a millennium on, the cart could, says Rosheim, not only rewrite the history of robotics but also bring another da Vinci to light: da Vinci the roboticist. "If it was simply a spring-powered cart, it would not be that big a deal," he says. "What's significant is that you can replace or change these cams and alter how it goes about its path – in other words, it's programmable in an analog, mechanical sense. It's the Disney animatronics of its day." The individual parts, interestingly, are not original to da Vinci – gears, cams, and the verge-and-foliot mechanism were all familiar concepts, particularly to clockmaking, the nanotech of da Vinci's day.

Indeed, as the historian Otto Mayr has noted, "clocks and automata, in short, tended to be very much the same thing"; clocks, in 16th-century dictionaries, were considered just one type of automata. But the possibility is that da Vinci married two ideas and created, in essence, a clock on wheels – turning the segmenting of time into the traversing of space – well before anyone else had thought of such a thing. No one could have done it as elegantly, in so compact a package, says Rosheim. "The robot cart is one of the most significant missing links in studying Leonardo. Suddenly, many drawings are making sense."

After weeks of peering at the faded filigree of ancient manuscripts, it's strange to see da Vinci's drawings in three dimensions. The models look at once primitive and complex, like out-of-time machines, steampunk for the Middle Ages. Rosheim had only one comment on the reconstruction: "They apparently didn't figure out how the escapement mechanism works, because theirs just kind of runs really fast and then runs out of steam." The model, along with another "top secret" reconstruction, will accompany Rosheim's book, Leonardo's Lost Robots. His model backs up the theory of his original drawing.

He said, "As you see in Codex Atlanticus folio 812, Leonardo has one half of the right large gear with cams and the other half with none. This generates a left-right zigzag motion."

In 2005, the Biochemical Engineering Faculty at the University of Connecticut began a recreation of the basic structure of da Vinci's original robot. Their design will incorporate 21st century technology including vision, speech recognition, and voice command, computer-integrated movements, and a more advanced body structure. The robot will also possess a mobile neck and have the capacity to follow moving objects with its eyes. The recreation will operate in two modes, one which will respond to computer commands and the other to spoken commands. Da Vinci's original pulleys and gears will be utilized in conjunction with muscle models to imitate natural human movements. Leonardo's programmable automaton is the first record of a programmable analog computer in the history of civilization. Leonardo's first design effort in planning automata culminating in his fabulous robot knight, of about 1495, a practical demonstration piece based on his pioneering study of biomechanics. Leonardo's sophisticated use of mechanisms at a very early age further highlights his talent. The correct reconstruction of this work will continue to demand expert knowledge in several and widely diverse fields.

Book of Enoch

The book of Enoch is an Apochryphal book of the Old Testament, written in Hebrew about a century before Christ. The original version was lost about the end of the fourth century, and only fragments remained, but Bruce the traveller brought back a copy from Abyssinia, in 1773 in Ethiopia, probably made from the version known to the early Greek fathers. The book told of the order of angels called "Watchers," or "The Sleepless Ones." The leader was the chief of the giant (Nephilim) called Semjaza or Samyasa (also known as Azazel, one of the Hebrews' principal demons), is equivalent to Ahriman, Satan or Lucifer who led 200 Watchers down to Earth to take wives from among the daughters of men and their offspring called the Anakim. It was from such a union that the Nephilim, the heroes of old, as well as the ancient practitioners of sorcery, were born. The fallen angels taught their wives to cast various spells and to practice the arts of enchantment.

The book says: "that there were angels who consented to fall from, heaven that they might have intercourse with the daughters of earth. For in those days the sons of men having multiplied, there were born to them daughters of great beauty. And when the angels, or sons of heaven, beheld them, they were filled with desire; wherefore they said to one another: Come let us choose wives from among the race of man, and let us beget children'. Their leader Samyasa, answered thereupon and said: 'Perchance you will be wanting in the courage needed to fulfill this resolution, and then I alone shall be answerable for your fall.' But they swore that they would in no wise repent and that they would achieve their whole design. Now there were 200 who descended on Mount Hermon

121

(or Armon), and it was from this time that the mountain received its designation, which signifies Mount of the Oath.

Hereinafter follow the names of those angelic leaders who descended with this object: Samyasa, chief among all, Urakabarameel, Azibeel, Tamiel, Ramuel, Danel, Azkeel, Sprakuyal, Asael, Armers, Batraal, Ananc, Zavebe, Sameveel, Ertrael, Turel, Jomiael, Arizial. They took wives with whom they had intercourse, to whom also they taught Magic, the art of enchantment and the diverse properties of roots and trees. Just as Prometheus presented man with fire, Samyasa did not neglect human men, so they teach them how to create weapons and tools of destruction. He released to humankind the secrets of metallurgy, the manufacture of weapons and jewelry, and the use of antimony in art and medicine. He also taught women the art of cosmetics to seduce men. For these transgressions, the archangels Michael, Gabriel, Raphael and Uriel appeal to God to punish the offspring of the Nephilim and the fallen angels on earth. God sent Uriel to instruct Noah to build a large ship and tell him of the coming Great Flood (cataclysm) to cleanse the world from evil and then God condemned Azazel to remain forever bound in the desert of Dûdâêl.

Based on ancient texts and manuscripts, Mount Hermon is where it all happened. Ancient legends attribute a sacred character to Mount Hermon. Hermon is also the mountain of God, called Bashan. Modern surveys have located more than twenty temples on Mount Hermon, an unprecedented number in comparison with other regions of the Phoenician coast. The Mount abounds with shrines to the Canaanite goddess Asherah or Astarte. This led the Church father Jerome to write that Hermon was an anathema, by which he meant a forbidden place.

The name Hermon derives from the Laconian dialect for stone heap. Archeologists discovered such a heap of hewn stone within the ruins of a circular wall on one of the three secondary peaks. In fact, all monumental walls and buildings built of ashlars, or cut stones, represent Hermon. He is also equivalent to Hermes, or Thoth-Hermes, the biblical Ham.

A translation of the *Book of Enoch* was published by Archbishop Lawrence in 1821, the Etheopic text in 1838, and there is a good edition by Dillman (1851). Philippi and Ewald have also written special works on the subject and the only known statute of the leader of the Watchers is in the choir of Rosslyn Chapel, in Scotland.

(or Amnon), and it was from this time that the mountain received its designation, which signifies Mount of the Oath,

Black Madonna of Czestochowa

Of the more than 400 images of the Black Madonna or Black Virgin known worldwide, the image of Our Lady in Czestochowa, Poland, has received the most recent recognition because of the personal devotion displayed toward this religious icon by Pope John Paul II (1920–2005). The pope, a native of Poland, prayed before the

Madonna of Czestochowa in 1979, several months after his election to the Chair of Peter, and he is known to have made subsequent visits in 1983 and in 1991. The reports of miracles and healings attributed to Our Lady of Czestochowa (also known as Our Lady of Jasna Gora) through the centuries are numerous. They include Our Lady greatly enhancing the ability of a small group of Polish defenders to protect her sanctuary from an army of Swedish invaders in 1655 and her holy apparition appearing to disperse an invading army of Russians in 1920. Records of such spectacular acts of intervention and dramatic cures are kept in the archives of the Pauline Fathers at Jasna Gora, the monastery site in which the portrait was housed for six centuries. The Black Madonna of Czestochowa is of such antiquity that its origins are unknown.

Tradition has it that St. Luke, the "beloved physician," painted the portrait of Jesus's mother on the cedar wood table at which she took her meals. Two centuries later, during her visit to the Holy Land,

St. Helena (c. 248 - c. 328), the Queen-Mother of Emperor Constantine (d. 337), is said to have discovered the portrait and brought it to Constantinople in the fourth century.

Five centuries later, determined to save the image of the Madonna from the repeated invasions of the Tartars, St. Ladislaus (1040–1095) took the portrait to Opala, Poland, the city of his birth, for safekeeping. Regretfully, not long after its move, a disrespectful Tartar arrow managed to find its way to the Madonna's throat, inflicting a scar that still remains visible. In 1430, Hussite thieves stole the portrait and broke it into three pieces. Contemporary scholar Leonard Moss has argued against a vast antiquity for the Black Madonna of Czestochowa, claiming that the figure of the woman in the portrait was painted in a distinctly thirteenth- or fourteenth century Byzantine style. Janusz Pasierb, another scholar who examined the portrait, counters such an assertion, stating that the image was "painted virtually new" in 1434 because of the extensive damage that the portrait had suffered at the hands of vandals.

Another aspect of the mystery of Our Lady of Czestochowa and all the other Black Madonnas that has puzzled many individuals is why they are portrayed with such dark skin tones. Some scholars answer this by stating that it wasn't until the onset of the Renaissance in the fourteenth century that Jesus, Mary, and Joseph began being portrayed with pale skin, blue eyes, and blond or reddishblond hair. Prior to that period, the Holy Family and the apostles were most often depicted as semitic people whose dark skin tones reflected the hot arid climate in which they lived. If the Black Madonna of Czestochowa was truly a portrait of Mary that had been painted from life by the apostle Luke, he would surely have captured a woman with olive or dark brown skin and black or brown hair.

Other researchers into the mystique of the Black Madonna state that the reasons that the Roman Catholic Church in general has not warmly embraced such depictions of the Holy Mother or Virgin Mary are because they fear that such representations are actually paying tribute to the ancient goddesses and Earth mothers and that these images perpetuate strains of pagan worship of the female principle. For example, church scholars point out that St. Germain de Pres, the oldest church in Paris (Par-isis, the Grove of Isis), was built in 542 on the site of a former temple dedicated to Isis. Isis had been the patron goddess of Paris until Christianity replaced her with St. Genevieve. Within the church of St. Germain de Pres, however, parishioners worshipped a black statue of Isis until it was destroyed in 1514. Christianity warred against goddess worship from the days of the apostles when St. Paul (d. 62 – 68 C.E.) found to his great frustration that his message was being shouted down by the crowds at Ephesus who pledged their obeisance to Diana. Until they had been romanized and westernized, Diana/Artemis, together with the other two preeminent goddesses of the East, Isis and Cybele, were first represented as black madonnas. And before the people of the East bent their knees to Diana, Isis, and Cybele, they had worshipped the Great Mother as Inanna in Sumeria, as Ishtar in Babylonia, and as Astarte among the Hebrews.

Most scholars agree that among the first images of the Black Madonna and her son were representations of Isis and Horus. The Black Madonna may also refer to Mary Magdalene, who, in the traditions of many Christian sects, such as the Gnostics, was the wife of Jesus (c. 6 B.C.E. – c. 30 C.E.) In this interpretation of the events that occurred after Jesus' death at the hands of the Romans, Mary brought the cup used at the Last Supper – the Holy Grail – from Palestine to southern France, where it would eventually be guarded by the Knights Templar.

There is also a belief that Mary arrived in France carrying within her womb a child fathered by Jesus of Nazareth, who then became the progenitor for the royal family of France. For those who hold such beliefs, the Holy Grail is but a metaphor for Mary Magdalene's womb, which carried the true blood of Jesus in the person of his unborn son. Therefore, many of the depictions of the Black Madonna and child throughout the regions of southern France and Spain may be regarded as images of Mary Magdalene carrying the infant son of Jesus rather than the Virgin Mary carrying the infant Jesus.

Mystery of the Bog Bodies

Bog bodies are often found in the peat bogs of Northern Europe, from Ireland and the United Kingdom to the Netherlands, Denmark, and Germany over the past 300 years. The first recorded specimen was uncovered in 1791 in the Netherlands, and hundreds more have

been discovered since then as peat in the ancient sphagnum bogs has been mined over the years. As diggers work their way through a level of peat, a shovel will hit something that feels different, or perhaps a hand will come tumbling out of the ragged mass of plant material. Further investigation in the surrounding peat can bring a whole body into view. Most of the corpses are those of ancient Europeans – Celts and Germanic tribesmen who lived in the northern forests while the Romans lived in the lands to the south. The majority of these bog mummies or bog bodies date to between the first century B.C. and the fourth century A.D., though the oldest dates from the Mesolithic period (about 10,000 years ago). They are commonly given names related to the locale where they are discovered.

There are also some medieval and modern examples. The astonishing preservative powers of the bogs have prevented the decay of these ancient remains so effectively that, although the skeleton does not usually survive, we have the skin, internal organs, stomach (sometimes including the remains of the last meal), eyes, brains, and hair. Bog waters are suffused with tannins (organic acids) and even aldehydes, which act to kill microorganisms, inhibit bacterial decomposition, and promote the preservation of soft tissues. So rich are bog waters in dissolved tannins from the plants within the bog that the waters are often stained brown by the tannin. This same brown appears in the skins of bog bodies. The ambient chemicals in a bog can act much like the tannin derived from bark that leather workers use to tan hides. The bog bodies are essentially tanned into leather by their immersion, which accounts for their leathery appearance as modern specimens. But how and why did these people meet their death in remote bogs thousands of years ago? One thing we do know is that a large amount of the bodies recovered show signs of extreme violence, including signs of torture and murder. More than 80 bodies have been recovered from the bogs of Ireland in the past two centuries, seven of which have been radiocarbon dated. Unlike the rest of Northern Europe, the majority of these bodies belong to the late medieval or post-medieval period, though there are some from the Iron Age.

The earliest recorded find of a bog bodies in Europe is the Kibbelgaarn body in the Netherlands, unearthed in 1791. In the 19th and 20th centuries there were hundreds of discoveries made in Holland. Gallagh Man is one Iron Age example, radiocarbon dated to between 470 and 120 B.C., found by the O'Kelly family in 1821 at Gallagh, near Castleblakeney, County Galway. Gallagh Man was naked but a deerskin cloak tied at the throat with a band of willow rods, which may have been used as a strangling device. As with many other bog bodies that suffered violence, his hair had been cropped short. He may have been a criminal and suffered public execution, as the body had been staked to the ground with pointed wooden sticks, possibly to prevent his soul from escaping, a practice known from some Danish bog bodies.

In 1879 Huldremose Woman, found in a bog near Ramten, Jutland, Denmark, was discovered with two skin capes, a woollen skirt, a scarf, and a hair band. Examination of the body revealed the gruesome details that her arms and legs had been repeatedly hacked, one arm being cut completely off, before she was deposited in the peat. The woman met this brutal death sometime between 160 B.C. and A.D. 340.

Perhaps the most famous of these bog bodies is Tollund Man, found in May 1950, near the village of Tollund in Denmark, by two brothers cutting peat. When the men first glimpsed the face staring up at them, they thought it was a recent murder victim and immediately contacted the local police. But subsequent radiocarbon dating of Tollund Man's hair showed that he had died around 350 B.C. During the operation to remove the body from his resting place, one of the helpers collapsed and died of a heart attack. Perhaps, as the late Danish archaeologist P.V. Glob suggested, this was a case of the bog claiming a life for a life. Tollund Man's body had been arranged in a fetal position at the time of death, and was naked apart from a pointed skin cap and a hide belt. His hair had been cropped extremely short and there was stubble clearly visible on his chin and upper lip. A rope consisting of two leather thongs twisted together was pulled tightly around his neck, and it is believed that he was probably hanged or garroted using this rope.

Tests on the contents of his stomach reveal that Tollund Man's last meal had been a kind of vegetable and seed soup. An interesting fact about the soup is that its ingredients were a mixture of various kinds of wild and cultivated seeds, which included such an unusual quantity of knotweed that it must have been gathered especially for the purpose. One possibility is that the knotweed was an important ingredient in a ritual last meal that was somehow part of a sacred execution rite. This possibility is also suggested by the careful arrangement of the body and the fact that his eyes and mouth had been closed.

In 1952, near Windeby in Schleswig-Holstein, northern Germany, two bodies were found in a small bog. The first turned out to be male who had been strangled and then placed in the bog, the body held down by sharpened branches stuck firmly into the peat around him. The second body was that of a young girl of about 14 years of age, dating to the first century A.D. The girl had been blindfolded with a strip of cloth before being drowned in the bog, her body secured by a large stone and branches from a birch tree.

In 1978, the body of a girl aged between 25 and 30 was discovered in Meenybradden Bog, near Ardara, County Donegal, Ireland. The girl, with short cropped hair and eyelashes and eyelids still intact, had been wrapped in a woollen cloak and carefully placed in the grave. There was no evidence of violence on the body, which was radiocarbon dated to A.D. 1570. The cause of death, and why she was buried in the bog, is still a mystery.

128

Around 1980s, Lindow Man was unearthed. The body is naked but with an arm band made of fox fur and a thin rope around his neck. Lindow Man had been in his 20s when he died between A.D. 50 and A.D. 100. Examination of the body revealed that he had been hit twice on the crown of his head, probably with an axe, with sufficient force to detach chips of his skull into his brain. He had also been strangled using the leather garrote still remaining around his neck, and there was a gash on the throat, which may indicate that his throat had been cut. His hair had been trimmed (using scissors) two or three days before he met his death. The contents of his stomach included burned bread and traces of pollen from mistletoe, a plant sacred to the Celts. Celtic scholar and archaeologist Dr. Anne Ross believes that the threefold death suffered by Lindow Man, along with the blackened crust in his stomach, and the traces of mistletoe, suggest that the man was the victim of a Druidic sacrifice.

Two Irish bog bodies were found in 2003. The first was discovered in Clonycavan, County Meath, north of Dublin called the Clonycavan Man and the second in Croghan, County Offaly, just 25 miles away. Old Croghan Man, as he has become known, was in his mid-20s, a giant at around 6-feet 6-inches tall. He has been dated between 362 B.C. and 175 B.C.

Clonycavan Man, a young male around 5-feet 2-inches tall, dates from between 392 B.C. and 201 B.C. In common with other bog bodies, they appear to have been brutally tortured before their deaths, probably as ritual sacrifices. While Old Croghan Man's nipples had been cut and he had been stabbed in the ribs. A cut on his arm indicates that he had tried to defend himself during the attack. There were also holes in both his upper arms, where a hazel rope withy had been passed through to bind him. He was later decapitated and dismembered before being buried in the bog. In contrast to his violent end, Croghan Man's body revealed that he had well-manicured nails and relatively smooth hands, which indicate somebody who had probably never performed any manual work; perhaps he was a priest or a member of the aristocracy. Clonycavan Man suffered a massive wound to the head, caused by a heavy axe that shattered his skull, and also several other injuries on his body. One particularly distinctive feature was his unusual raised hairstyle, for which he had used a kind of Iron Age hair gel, actually a form of resin that had probably come from south-western France or Spain.

A more recent find from northern Germany, from Uchte, Lower Saxony, was at first thought to be the body of a teenage murder victim. But when scientists reexamined the body in January of 2005 it was identified as a young girl aged between 16 and 20, who had been deposited in the bog in about 650 B.C. She subsequently became known as the Girl of the Uchter Moor. Even her hair had been preserved, though archaeologists weren't sure whether it was originally blonde or black, as the peat turns all hair reddish.

Ned Kelly, keeper of Irish antiquities at the National Museum of Ireland, has developed a theory to explain why 40 bodies discovered in Irish bogland were made along tribal, political, and royal boundaries. His belief is that the burials are offerings to fertility gods by kings to guarantee a successful reign. This is certainly a possible explanation for many of the Irish bog bodies, but what of the rest of Northern Europe? The variety of different ways in which many of these people were killed would suggest something more than murder, probably some kind of ritual sacrifice.

The ancient Roman historian Tacitus wrote Germania, a contemporary account of the German tribes in the first century A.D., in which he described the Germans' capital punishment of criminals and outcasts by staking them in the bogs. He mentions some interesting customs connected with crime and punishment in their culture, including how "cowards, shirkers, and those guilty of unnatural vices" were forced down into the bog under a wicker hurdle. He also states that adulterous wives were stripped naked, had their heads shaved, and were turned out of the house and flogged through the village. There are certainly indications from Tacitus that suggest that many of the victims in the bogs had broken some law or taboo of the society for which they were executed. It is obvious that there can never be one single explanation for the gruesome but compelling mystery of the bog bodies, considering the vast array of possible theories.

Dorchester Pot

The Dorchester Pot was a metal vase that was recovered in two pieces after an explosion used to break up rock at Meeting House Hill, in Dorchester, Massachusetts in 1852. According to text reprinted from the Boston Transcript, a local paper, in the June 5, 1852 Scientific American, the two pieces were found, loose among debris thrown out by the explosion. Apparently, it was inferred from the locations of the two pieces of this pot among the explosion debris that this pot had been blasted from solid puddingstone (conglomerate), which is part of the Roxbury Conglomerate, from about 15 feet below the surface of Meeting House Hill.

The Roxbury Conglomerate, from which this pot is alleged to have come, has been dated as having accumulated between 570 and 593 million years ago and during the Ediacaran Period. It accumulated at the bottom of a deep rift basin, which was filled with marine water, within either glaciomarine or submarine fan and slope environments. Typically, tectonism has flattened, stretched, indented, and fractured the pebbles and associated matrix of the Roxbury Conglomerate to the point that it often has the appearance of flow structure.

The bell-shaped vessel was described as being about 4.5 inches (11.5 cm) high, 6.5 inches (16.5 cm) in diametre as the base and 2.5 inches (6.4 cm) in diametre at the top. The body of this object was said to resemble zinc alloyed with silver in colour. It reportedly exhibited floral designs on its side and a wreath or vine design around its lower part, which were both inlaid with silver. The primary source of information about this object, provides neither any picture of nor age estimate for the Dorchester Pot.

The Dorchester Pot is often discussed as an Out-of-place artefact by various popular books and articles about unsolved mysteries, alternative science, and different types of creationism. For example, a chapter on the "PureInsight" web page, provides without any attribution, a picture of an unknown object from an unknown source, showing what they apparently believe the Dorchester Pot looked like. It also provides without any explanation an age of 100,000 years for this artefact. As part of a short description, an identical image of the Dorchester Pot appears on page 46 of a 1985 Reader's Digest Association book. They do not provide any estimate of the age of the Dorchester Pot. The source that they credit for their photograph of the Dorchester Pot is Brad Steiger's "World's Before Our Own." Michael Cremo, a well-known Hindu creationist, claims that the Dorchester Pot is evidence for the "presence of artistic metal workers in North America over 600 million years ago." Some Young Earth creationists regard the Dorchester Pot as having been manufactured by an ancient civilization that predated the Noachian Flood.

Baghdad Battery:
The Missing Artefact

The Baghdad Battery, sometimes referred to as the Parthian Battery, is the common name for a number of artefacts created in Mesopotamia, possibly during the Parthian or Sassanid period (the early centuries AD). Some researchers have seen it in ancient Egyptian wall carvings or in ancient texts evidence for ancient electricity. Though these claims generally lack physical proof, there is one particular ancient artefact that is believed by some scientists to be an example of an electrical power source. Despite its plain appearance, this small, undecorated jar may change the accepted view of the history of scientific discovery. The object, thought to be a 2,000 year-old electric battery, was found in 1936 by workers moving earth for a new railway in the area of Khujut Rabu, southeast of Baghdad. The battery appears to have been unearthed in a tomb of the Parthian Period (247 B.C – A.D.228).

The artefacts consist of ~130 mm (~5 inch) tall terracotta jars (with a one and a half inch mouth) containing a copper cylinder made of a rolled-up copper sheet, which houses a single iron rod and some fragment of asphalt. The asphalt had been used to seal the top and bottom of the copper cylinder, as well as to hold the iron rod in place in the centre of the cylinder. The use of an asphalt sealing indicated that the object had once contained liquid of some sort, as is also suggested by traces of corrosion on the copper tube, which was probably caused by an acidic agent, perhaps vinegar or wine. This has led some scholars to believe lemon juice, grape juice, or vinegar was used as an acidic agent to jump-start the electrochemical reaction with the two metals. At the top, the iron rod is isolated from the copper by bitumen plugs or stoppers, and both rod and cylinder fit snugly inside the opening of the jar which bulges outward towards the middle. The copper cylinder is not watertight, so when the jar was filled with a liquid containing the type of acid found in orange juice, this would surround the iron rod as well. The artefact had been exposed to the weather and had suffered corrosion, although mild given the presence of an electrochemical couple. Similar artefacts were found in the nearby cities of Seleucia (where the jar contained papyrus rolls) and Ctesiphon (Where it contained rolled bronze sheets).

In 1938, German archaeologist Wilhelm Konig, then director of the Baghdad Museum Laboratory, came upon the strange object, or a series of objects (accounts differ) in a box in the museum basement. After a close examination, he realized that the artefact closely resembles a galvanic cell, or a modern electrical battery. Konig subsequently published a paper suggesting that the object was an ancient battery, possibly used for electroplating (transferring a thin film of gold or silver from one surface to another) gold onto silver objects. He also theorized that several batteries could have been attached to each other to increase their output. The most conservative date for the battery is now thought to be somewhere between 250 B.C. and A.D. 640, but the first known electric battery, the Voltaic pile, was not invented by Italian physicist Alessandro Volta until 1800. König thought the objects might date to the Parthian period (between 250 BC and AD 224).

However according to Dr. St. John Simpson of the Near Eastern department of the British Museum, their original excavation and context were not well recorded, so evidence for this date range is very weak. Most of the components of the objects are not particularly amenable to advanced dating methods. The ceramic pots could be analysed by thermoluminescence dating, but this has apparently not yet been done; in any case, it would only date the firing of the pots, which is not necessarily the same as when the complete artefact was assembled.

Another possibility would be ion diffusion analysis, which could indicate how long the objects were buried. So if this was a primitive battery, where did the ancient Parthians acquire the knowledge to assemble it, and how did it work? After reading Konig's paper, Willard F.M. Gray, an engineer at the General Electric High Voltage Laboratory in Pittsfield, Massachusetts, decided to construct and test a replica of the ancient battery. When he filled the clay jar with grape juice, vinegar, or copper sulphate solution, he found that it generated about one and a half to two volts of electricity. In 1978, Egyptologist Dr. Arne Eggebrecht, at the time director of the Roemer and Pelizaeus Museum in Hildesheim, Germany, constructed a replica of the Baghdad Battery and filled it with grape juice. This replica generated 0.87 volts, which he used to electroplate a silver statuette with gold; the layer deposited being a mere 1/10,000 of a millimetre thick. As a result of this experiment. Eggebrecht speculated that many ancient items in museums that are presumed to be manufactured from gold may instead be gold-plated silver. More replicas of the Baghdad artefact were made in 1999 by students under the supervision of Dr. Marjorie Senechal, professor of mathematics and the history of science at Smith College in the Massachusetts. The students filled one replica jar with vinegar, and it produced 1.1 volts.

Judging by these experiments, the Baghdad Battery was obviously able to produce a small current, but what would it have been used for? Even if it is accepted that the "Baghdad batteries" were in fact electrical devices, this provides no evidence of any real knowledge of electrical phenomena. Thales of Miletus was aware of electrostatic phenomena produced by amber, without possessing any theoretical explanation. As electrical power supplies, the "Baghdad batteries" would be inefficient when compared to modern devices. Luigi Galvani formulated a similar electrochemical couple experiment in the 1780s and, 20 years later, Alessandro Volta developed enough theory to convert Galvani's simple experiment into the efficient voltaic pile, producing around 30 volts of continuous current using devices which were much larger than known Baghdad relics. Within two or three more years Sir Humphry Davy was using voltaic piles that produced 1,000 volts and enough current to run an arc lamp. The most popular theory is the one originated by Konig, that when those cells were connected together in a series, the current generated would have been enough for electroplating metals. Konig found Sumerian copper vases plated with silver, dating back to 2500 B.C., which he speculated could have been electroplated using similar batteries to that discovered in Khujut Rabu, though no evidence of Sumerian batteries has ever been found. Konig pointed out that craftsmen in modern-day Iraq still use a primitive electroplating technique to coat copper jewelry with a fine layer of silver. He thought it possible that the method was in use in the Parthian period and had been passed on down the years.

In a slightly different form, the technique is known today in a process called gilding, where a layer of gold or silver is applied to a piece of jewelry. Another theory regarding the electrical use of the batteries is that they were used medicinally. Ancient Greek and Roman writings indicate that there was a fairly sophisticated knowledge of electricity in the ancient world. The Greeks mention how pain could be treated by applying electric fish to the feet; sufferers would stand on an electric eel until the inflamed foot become numb. Torpedo or electric rays possess two electric organs behind their eye, and discharge 50 to 200 volts at 50 amps, which they use as a weapon to stun small prey that swim above them.

The Roman writer Claudian described how a torpedo was caught on a bronze hook and emitted an effluence which spread through the water and up the line to give the fisherman a shock. It is recorded that Roman doctors would attach a pair of these electric rays onto patient's temples in order to treat a range of illnesses, from gout to headaches. Ancient Babylonian doctors are also known to have used electric fish as a local anesthetic.

The ancient Greeks also discovered one of the earliest examples of static electricity; when they rubbed amber (in Greek, electron) against a piece of fur, they found that amber would afterward attract feathers, dust particles, and pieces of straw. However, although the Greeks noticed this strange effect, they had no idea what caused it and probably regarded it as a mere curiosity. But not everyone is convinced of the practicality of the battery for the treatment of pain.

The main problem with the theory of medicinal use is the very low voltage the battery produces, which some doubt would have had any noticeable effect on anything other than very minor pain. Again though, if a series of these batteries were connected together, there could have been enough electricity generated. Staying with an medicinal/electrical explanation for the Baghdad Battery, Paul T. Keyser of the University of Alberts in Canada, has postulated another use for the battery based on finds of bronze and iron needles discovered with other battery-like devices unearthed at Seleucia, not far from Babylon. His suggestion, published in a 1993 paper, is that these needles may have been used for a kind of electro-acupuncture, a treatment already in use in China at the time.

Some researchers favour a ritual use for the Baghdad Battery. Dr. Paul Craddock, an expert in historical metallurgy from the Department of Scientific Research at the British Museum, has proposed that a group of these ancient cells connected together may have been concealed inside a metal statue. Worshippers coming into contact with the idol would get a small electric shock, similar to that of static electricity, possibly when giving the wrong answer to a question posed by the priest.

Perhaps this mysterious tingling effect would have been thought of by the worshippers as evidence of magic, and the power and mystique of the particular priest and temple would thus be greatly enhanced. Unfortunately, unless such statues are actually recovered, a ritual use for the cells remains just another fascinating theory. Despite the repeated tests with replicas of the Baghdad batteries, sceptics argue that there is no proof that they ever functioned as electric batteries. They note that the ancient people supposedly responsible for this technology, the Parthians, were known as great warriors, but not regarded for their scientific achievements.

Skeptics also point to the fact that despite the extensive historical records we have concerning this area and period, there is no mention of anything connected with electricity anywhere. There are also no archaeological finds from the Parthian period that have been proved to be electrogilded, and no evidence of wires, conductors, or more complete examples of ancient batteries. Some researchers have also disputed the results from experiments with replicas of the battery, claiming that they have been unable to duplicate the results themselves.

Dr. Arne Eggebrecht's experiments in particular, have come under fire. According to Dr. Bettina Schmitz, a researcher at Roemer and Pelizaeus Museum (the same institution where Eggebrecht did his 1978 experiments with reproductions of the battery), there are no photos or written documentation of the experiments which Eggebrecht undertook. A favoured alternative explanation of these sceptical of the electrical battery theory is that the jars acted as storage vessels for sacred scrolls, perhaps containing rituals of some sort written on organic material such as parchment or papyrus. If such organic materials had rotten away, the sceptics claim, they would leave a slightly acidic organic residue, which would explain the corrosion on the copper cylinder.

They believe that an asphalt seal such as that on the Baghdad battery, while not particularly practical for a Galvanic cell, would be perfect as a hermetic seal for storage over an extended period. That the Baghdad batteries would be inefficient compared to modern devices, even when several were connected together, is not in doubt. But the fact remains that the device does actually function as an electric cell. What is probable is that, similar to the ancient Greeks with amber, the makers of the object did not properly understand the principle involved. But this is not unusual.

Many innovations, such as gunpowder and herbal medicines, were developed before their fundamentals were soundly grasped. Nevertheless, even if the Baghdad artefact is one day proved to be an ancient electric battery, it would not be evidence of any genuine comprehension of electrical phenomena 2,000 years ago. The question now remains whether the Baghdad Battery was an isolated find. Can its manufacturers have been the only people in antiquity to discover – probably by accident – electricity? Obviously there is a need for further evidence, whether literary or archaeological, because based on current knowledge, it is likely that the battery is indeed a unique find. Tragically, in 2003, during the war in Iraq, the Baghdad Battery was looted from the National Museum, along with thousand of other priceless ancient artefacts. Its current whereabouts are unknown.

The Antikythera Mechanism

One day a Greek archaeologist named Spyridon Stais was carefully going through some of the material brought up from a shipwreck. The wreck had been found accidentally two years earlier in 1900 when a group of sponge divers had been blown off course and forced to anchor at a new location near the island of Crete at a place called Antikythera. There the sponge divers started conducting business as usual. Instead of finding sponges, however, they started bringing up bits of pottery and other very old artefacts. Amazingly, what the divers had happened upon was a Roman ship that floundered at sea an estimated 2000 years earlier.

The Greek government, anxious to recover what they could from the wreck, had employed the divers to take on the difficult job of bringing up artefacts from the bottom of the sea using the same methods they used to search for sponges: free dives with no breathing apparatus. It was a dangerous business. One diver died and another was permanently disabled. Still, the group managed to retrieve a treasure trove of historical objects.

One of the less impressive finds was the lump of material that Stais was looking at. It appeared to be a mass of wood which was now decaying since it had been brought to the surface and started drying out. The rot seemed to have exposed something that Stais hadn't seen before: a bit of metal. Not just a bit of metal, a bit of metal that was round with teeth. A gear. Stais couldn't believe his eyes. A metal gear from a shipwreck before the birth of Christ? What was this thing?

What Stais had stumbled upon was the remains of one of the world's oldest-geared devices – an analog computer – almost two millennia in age. Over the next century it would upset the archeological world's understanding about the kind of technology the ancients were capable of producing.

After Stais's discovery, speculation about what the device was used for echoed around the archeological world for decades. Scientists knew that the device seemed to have 32 interlocking gears and a hand crank, plus a display that showed information about the moon, sun and planets against a background of stars. The gears inside the mechanism were made of bronze and the whole device had apparently been mounted in a wooden box that measured about 13 inches high, 7 inches wide and 3 ½ inches deep. Unfortunately, much of the device however had been damaged by its time in the water, making it difficult to work out exactly how all the parts had been put together.

Efforts to figure out what the thing actually did received a boost in 1971 when the mechanism was X-rayed. This enabled scientists to count the teeth on each gear and then make detailed drawings to determine how it might have worked. In 1974, Derek de Solla Price, a historian at Yale University, who had been studying the mechanism for over twenty years, published a paper showing how he thought the mechanism operated. Price wrote that the existence of the device "requires us to completely rethink our attitudes toward ancient Greek technology." Price also built a reproduction of the device now housed at the National Museum in Athens.

Much of Price's work, however, was met with skepticism from other historians who advanced alternate, less-controversial theories. The existence of a device like the Antikythera Mechanism from this early a period in history simply did not match many historians' preconceived notions about the kind of technical expertise the ancients had. One skeptic, in a desperate attempt to explain how such a sophisticated object was found in the remains of a Roman ship, suggested that it was actually a device from the 18th century that had fallen overboard at some later date and onto the deck of the wreck.

Recent efforts to find out more about the device have been spearheaded by the Antikythera Mechanism Research Project, a consortium of several agencies, businesses and museums interested in finding out more about the object. The device was too fragile to be removed from its home at the National Archaeological Museum of Athens, so the Project constructed a 12-ton portable micro focus computerized tomographer that used high resolution X-rays to probe the object and create a 3-dimensional image. Two Hewlett-Packard scientists, also involved in the project, used a technique they developed involving a digital camera and fifty different lights to photograph details of the object that could not previously be seen. In 2006, the Project announced that with these tools almost 95 percent of the text engraved on the various parts of the device is now readable, giving scientists a much-improved understanding of its capabilities.

Much of what Price and other researchers surmised about the device seems to be true. The mechanism was clearly an analog computer designed to allow the operator to predict the future or past positions of the sun, moon, and probably some of the planets. On the front of the device were two dials marked with the zodiac and a solar calendar, with pointers for the Sun and Moon plus a display showing the phase of the moon. On the rear of the object was displayed information about the Saros cycle (a period of around 18 years used in eclipse prediction) and the Callippic cycle (a period of about 76 years) using two ingeniously designed spiral dials.

The capability of the machine has amazed scientists. It has an accuracy of one unit of error out of 860000. One researcher, Professor Mike Edmonds remarked, "This device is just extraordinary, the only thing of its kind. The design is beautiful, the astronomy is exactly right. The way the mechanics are designed just makes your jaw drop. Whoever has done this has done it extremely carefully."

Who built this ingenious device? Some have gone so far as to suggest it was the work of aliens. There is no real evidence for this, of course, and historical texts do have references to devices similar in design to the Antikythera Mechanism. The Roman historian Cicero wrote about a device supposedly constructed by the Greek philosopher Archimedes which was brought back to Rome by the Roman general Marcus Claudius Marcellus after he conqured Syracuse in 212 BC. According to Cicero, he received a demonstration of the device from a descendant of Marcellus and the object displayed the motions of the sun, moon and five planets. Cecero also mentions that a similar device was built by his friend Posidonius, another Greek philospher.

A millenium later the Persian scholar al-Biruni also described a device similar to the Antikythera Mechanism and included a diagram of it in a treatise written in AD 996. Though it was much simpler in design, historians have speculated that the object in the diagram was a direct descendant of the Antikythea device.

Price had a theory that the Antikythera Mechanism was constructed by the Greek astronomer Geminus on the Greek island of Rhodes around 87 BC. At the time the island was a centre of learning for astronomy and mechanical engineering. Engineers there were well-known for creating intricate automata (mechanical toys or tools that demonstrated basic scientific principles). The device could have found its way on board a Roman ship a decade later as part of a hoard of treasure being taken to Rome to be displayed in a triumphal parade for Julius Caesar.

This remains a matter of great speculation. Such a device would have been of great help to an astrologer in creating star charts. It could have also been used to correct calendars and set the dates of religious festivals. It might even have provided assistance in predicting what days eclipses were likely to occur.

We may never know exactly who built it or what it was used for. However, it remains a testament to the engineering skills of the ancients and a warning that despite all we know about history, there are still mysteries to be solved.

design to the Amulythera Mechanism. The Roman historian Cicero wrote about a device supposedly constructed by the Greek philosopher

Athanasius Kircher's Map of Atlantis

Kircher was a German polymath of the 17th century and also one of the scholars to seriously investigate the Atlantis legend. Initially skeptical, he cautiously began reconsidering its credibility while assembling mythic traditions of numerous cultures in various parts of the world about a great flood. His research led him to the immense collection of source materials at the Vatican Library, where, as Europe's foremost scholar, its formidable resources were at his disposal. It was here that he discovered a single piece of evidence which proved to him that the legend of Atlantis was actually fact. Athanasius Kircher, was born on 2 May in either 1601 or 1602 in Geisa, Buchonia, near Fulda, currently Hesse, Germany, this Jesuit priest was also a pioneering mathematician, physicist, chemist, linguist, and

archaeologist; the first to study phosphorescence; inventor of, among numerous futuristic innovations, the slide projector and a prototype of the microscope. The founding father of scientific Egyptology, he was the first serious investigation of temple hieroglyphs.

In 1665 Kircher found a well-preserved, treated-leather map purporting to show the configuration and location of Atlantis among the relatively few surviving documents from Imperial Rome in Vatican Library. The map was not Roman, but brought in the first century A.D. to Italy from Egypt, where it had been executed. It survived the demise of Classical Times, and found its way into the Vatican Library. Kircher copied it precisely, adding only a visual reference to the New World, and published it in his book, Mundus Subterraneus: The Subterranean World, in 1665. His caption states it is "a map of the island of Atlantis originally made in Egypt after Plato's description," which suggests it was created sometime following the 4th century B.C., perhaps by a Greek mapmaker attached to the Ptolemies. More probably, the map's first home was the Great Library of Alexandria, where numerous books and references to Atlantis were lost, along with another million plus volumes, when the institution was burned by religious fanatics. In relocating to Rome, the map escaped that destruction.

Similar to modern conclusions forced by current understanding of geology in the Mid-Atlantic Ridge, Kircher's map depicts Atlantis, not as a continent, but an island about the size of Spain and France combined. It shows a large, centrally located volcano, most likely meant to represent Mount Atlas, together with six major rivers, something Plato does not mention. Kritias describes large rivers on the island of Atlantis, but does not indicate how many.

Although the map vanished after Kircher's death in 1680, it was the only known representation of Atlantis to have survived the Ancient World. Thanks to his research and book, it survives today in a close copy. Kircher was the first to publish a map of Atlantis, probably the most accurate of its kind to date. Curiously, it is depicted upside down, contrary to maps in both his day and ours. Yet, this apparent anomaly is proof of the map's authenticity, because Egyptian mapmakers, even as late as Ptolemaic times, designed their maps with the Upper Nile Valley located in the south ("Upper" refers to its higher elevation) at the top, because the river's headwaters are located in the Sudan.

144